"Romulous and Remus" (c)apostolos peter
kouroumalis(toly A.K) 2014

"Toxicity"
You lost that certain
Something
When you said goodbye
To me.

Cause im a howlin nightmare
And i ain't ever comin' back!

Nobody knows
The trouble i seen.
Nobody knows
Or walked in my shoes.

Cause im a howlin nightmare
And i ain't ever comin' back!

Been a long way from nowhere
On a long beaten track.

"Play it cool"- from bad seed

Their games are stealing
and lusting and they
keep track by the sin.

They stood like Obsidian
Idols, all dark, all
Glowering, all
Making that sound...

Young Johnny Broom
Had it all figured.
Their were easier ways
to get the fast
Buck and a cheap thrill.

Teenage Terror

She and her fifteen
year old girlfriend
Had identified 37 men with
whom they had intimate relations

Hell to pay!
Gang Rumble!
Innocent oversight?
Maybe ruthless exploitation?
Perhaps...

I live with regret
Not recognizing the faces
Out of the drum
Into the dark
Sphere solar rythms
While they check out
The reflexes.
Show me what you can do with your hands and orifices.
Sweet spasms of consciousness
Show me another glance into your soul.

A winters warm night.

Anathema she held me while my mind
melted under synthetic intoxication,
my lungs collapsing and my chest heaving.
From the long stare, ,my physical reality
spilling out into the dream.
She giggles softly-orixification.
The butcher knife dissects my brain.

A winters warm night.

"without a succubus"

A man sits
in a coffee shop
a lonely tear drop
ready to jump.
Yesterday, was better
at around one a.m.

Live life on the open road
Spiralling-murder,
Ravager of worlds
Through the open gate, gazing
Upon stragling ballads-unfolding.

The apple crumble mom baked.
Depressing earthquake
In her belly-no baby.
(sample:don't you baby me buster!)
Can't kill white fascist t.v.
Causing consumption
In the aqua lung of
Disease.
The turtle licked
The toads spine and
Got a jolt of
The morning.
Gotta bathe in milky
loser ode to nothin'!

"Back to you"
The planet ready to rumble
You know its on go
Too many to stumble
There, waiting
For what i surely don't know.

There were times i dreamed
You and i were
once again.

Now i wonder but i
Surely dont't know.

Take a srep back from the bloody refrain
We don't live in a glass house
We ask ourselves again

I want you so bad
I surely don't know
Hunker in deep and
Avoid the words that rhyme with id.

Now and then you wonder
But i surely don't know.
Rude pointy finger
People doin their best.
But i surely don't know.

"represent"
 W survived fire and flood.
And all of gods evil and sin.

We awake to the day again.
Whats a stone throw away.
Asorcerers wand astray.
Spreading magic and love.

You look into the Genies eye and hoof.
But never klnow how long it will last.you can drink a thouseand drinks and still not know.
What bag of tricks are in store
As the needle hits the turntable
The centrifuge on fire again.
Drink deep into apollos idle grind.
The hive mind
Too big to justify.

The world died with walt simonson
And is controlled by r.k. chaos
And we will wonder how long it will last
And all of gods wrath and sin
When you look into the mirror
And not see that its you.
Squirming in a psychotic realm.
Wanting to belong,
Without sounding like a soap opera company man.
When your eyes look like bugs and your antennas your flow.
Your larvae wonder, wickeerd evermore.
But youre deep in the thiuck of it
And the now doesn't matter,
With your fingers rubbed rawfrom the grind
And your back numb to the pain.
Get up and breath all the days begin anew.
You could drink an thousand drinks of gruel and not know
Still you ask for reason again.

`Todays coffee`
Do you want art
To make you a million
Use someone elses tank to destroyÉ

Itsa relative,
To a given time and situation.
When the worlds insane
But when youre on the mind
Tha makes go.
The puritains beat
You down,
Youll know
Its started again.

War and hunger, for tyhe
Masses.
Plague and strife,
In dark places.

Tadays a downer,
The patty wagons wheel
Spins outr classes.
Drink in deep
For the brave new world.

The worms delight,
That flowered into maggots

Go to hell,
We are all sinners.
Once you accept
We are all asses.
There you sit all prim and proper,
Powder you nose
For the ghost,
Of anathema

Voodoo
Beats, a new day is dawning
You punch the clock,
For the man to hunt down a luxury cruis e liner.

Takle care my friend
Im burning all the art
You pulled out to bring life
To the undead coprpse of civilization,
Of which we`ll eternally lie.

"Arrested Decay"
 Well i travelled all
The way to Tennessee
And never saw the pyramids staring at me.

Saw a fire pit the
Size of kalamazoo
To roast a pig
The size of me

Arrested decay on the highway.

A rotten Ford,
In a farmers field.
And an old sign that said
For sale-the universe and
A milkshake.
I made my way p[ast car crashes an
Tornbado thrown asphalt,
Only to come back to
Kalamazoo

Arrested decy on
The highway
Where youre moneys as good ass green
It'll ricochet

Slap that bass and and a speed cap
Or two
The rivers edge awaits.
On a blanket
Built for two
Where tuplips grow and fade

Arrested decay on the highway.

Paintings: apostoly peter kouroumalis(toly a.k.)
2013-2014

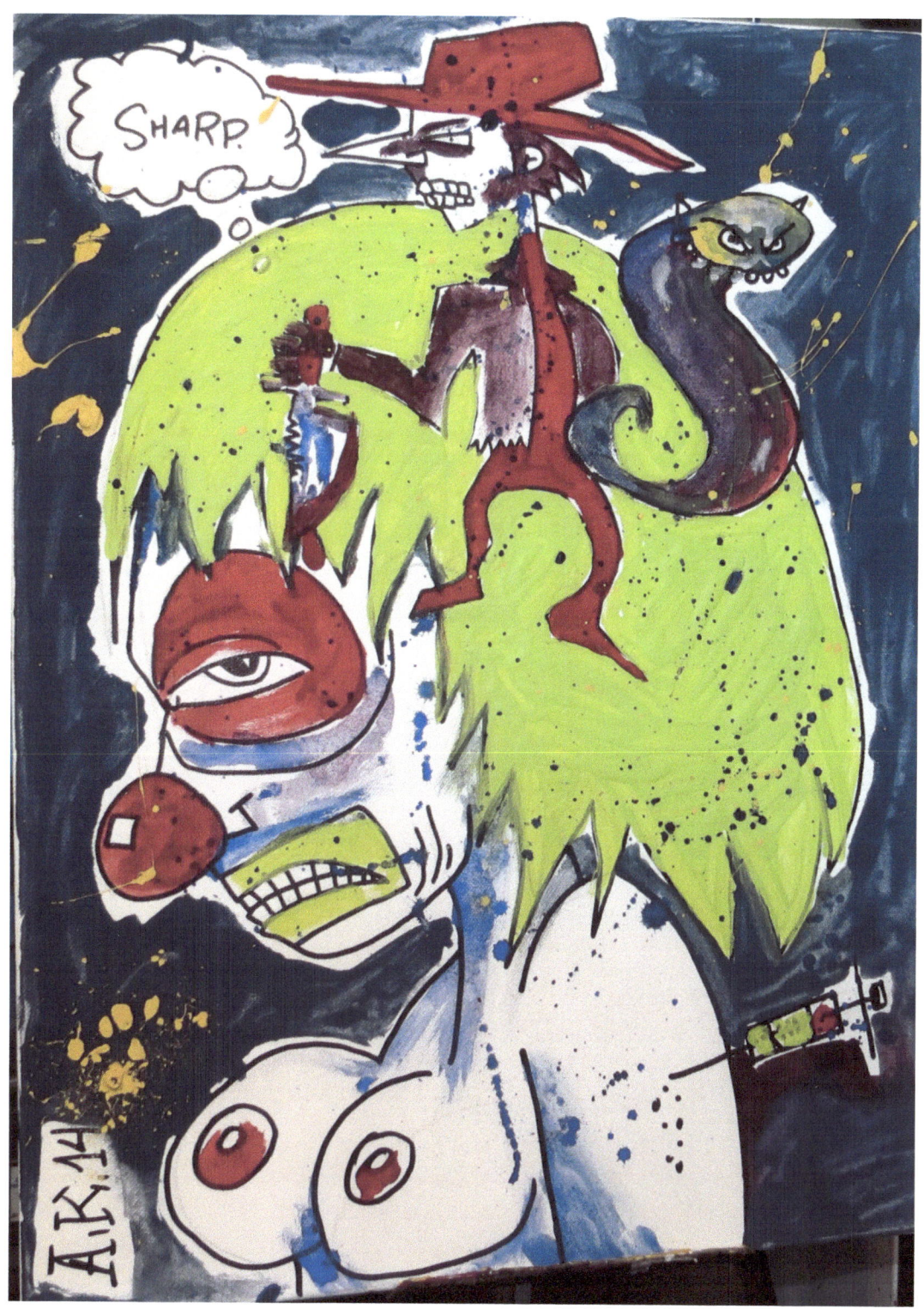

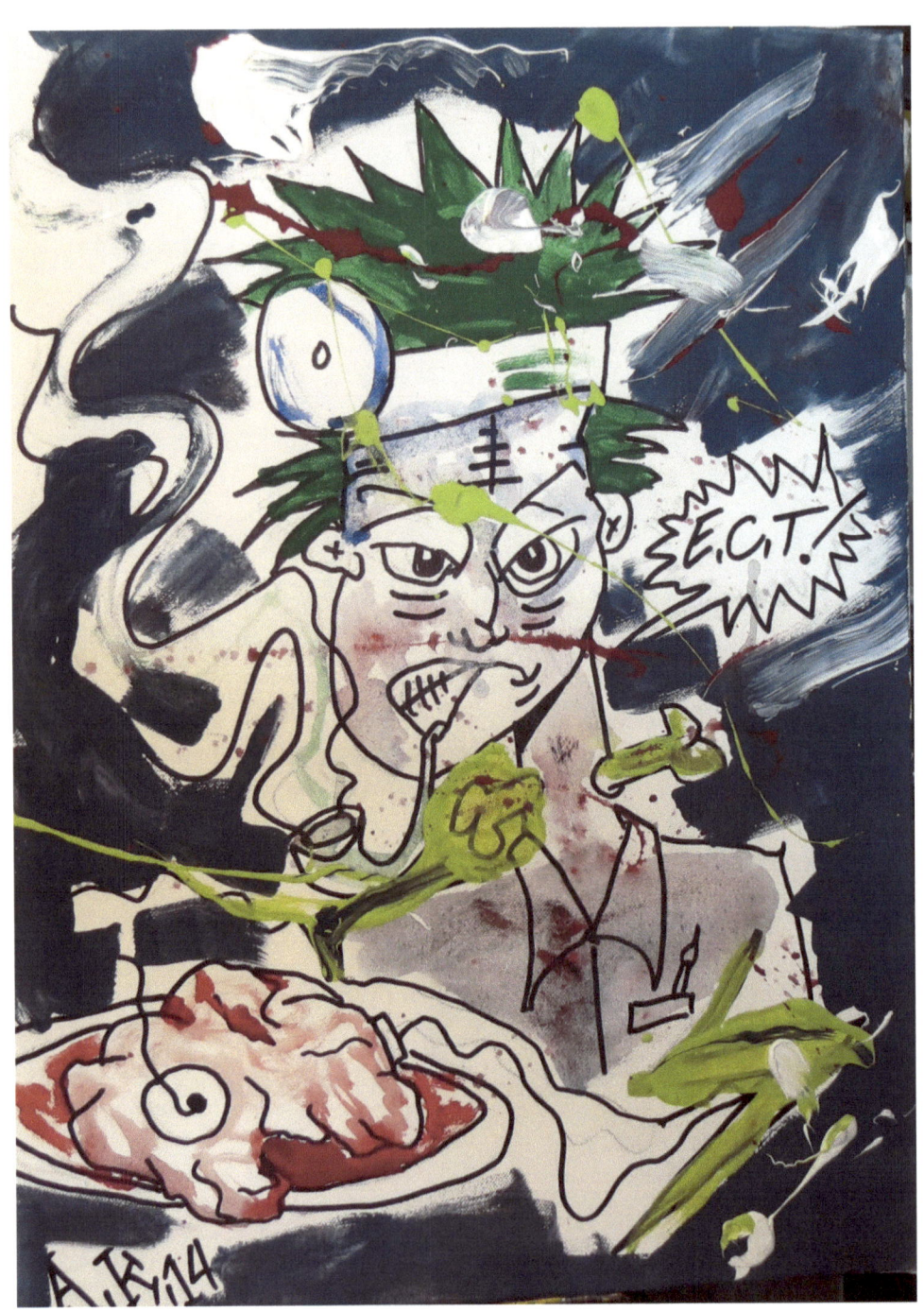

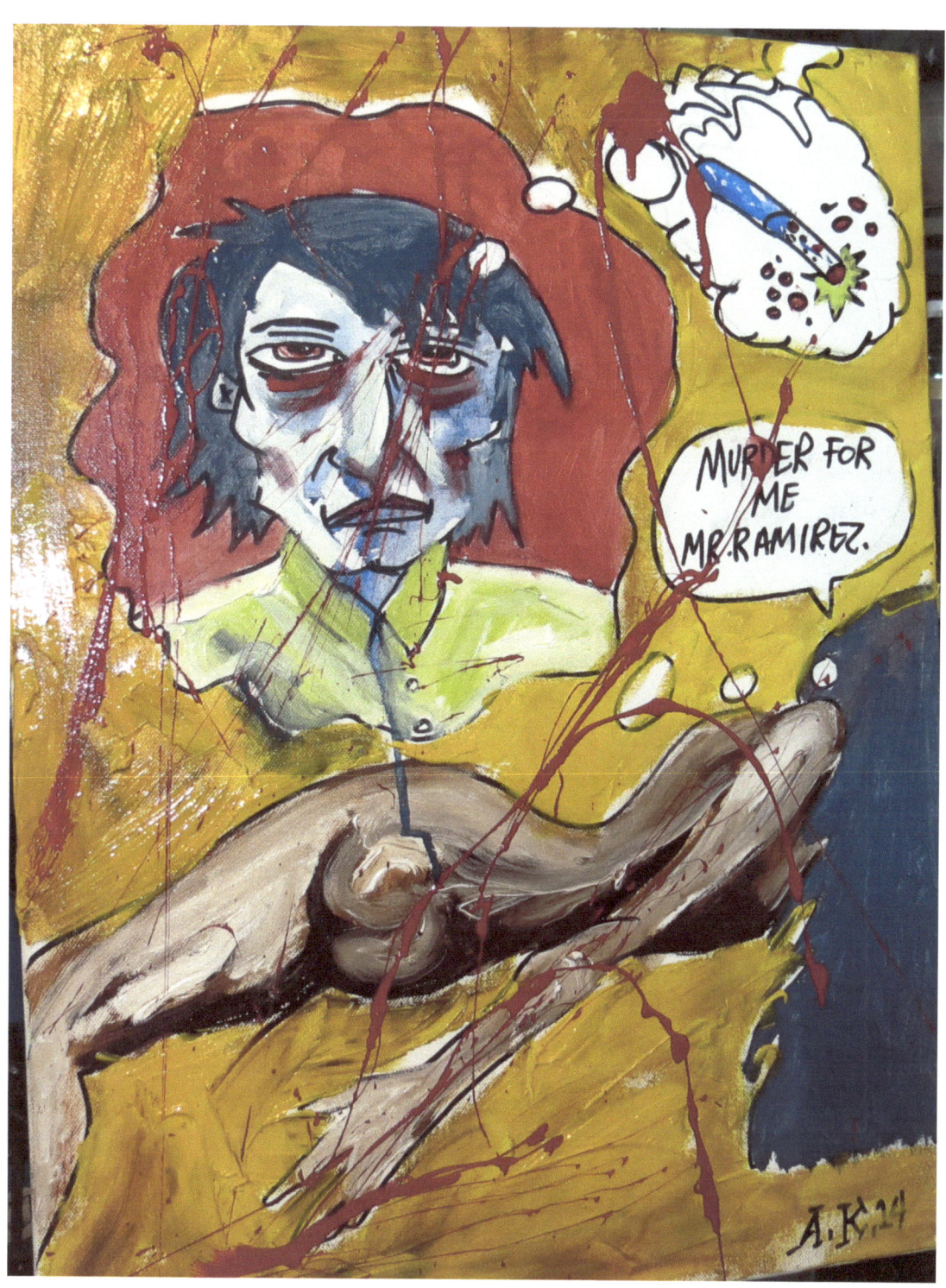

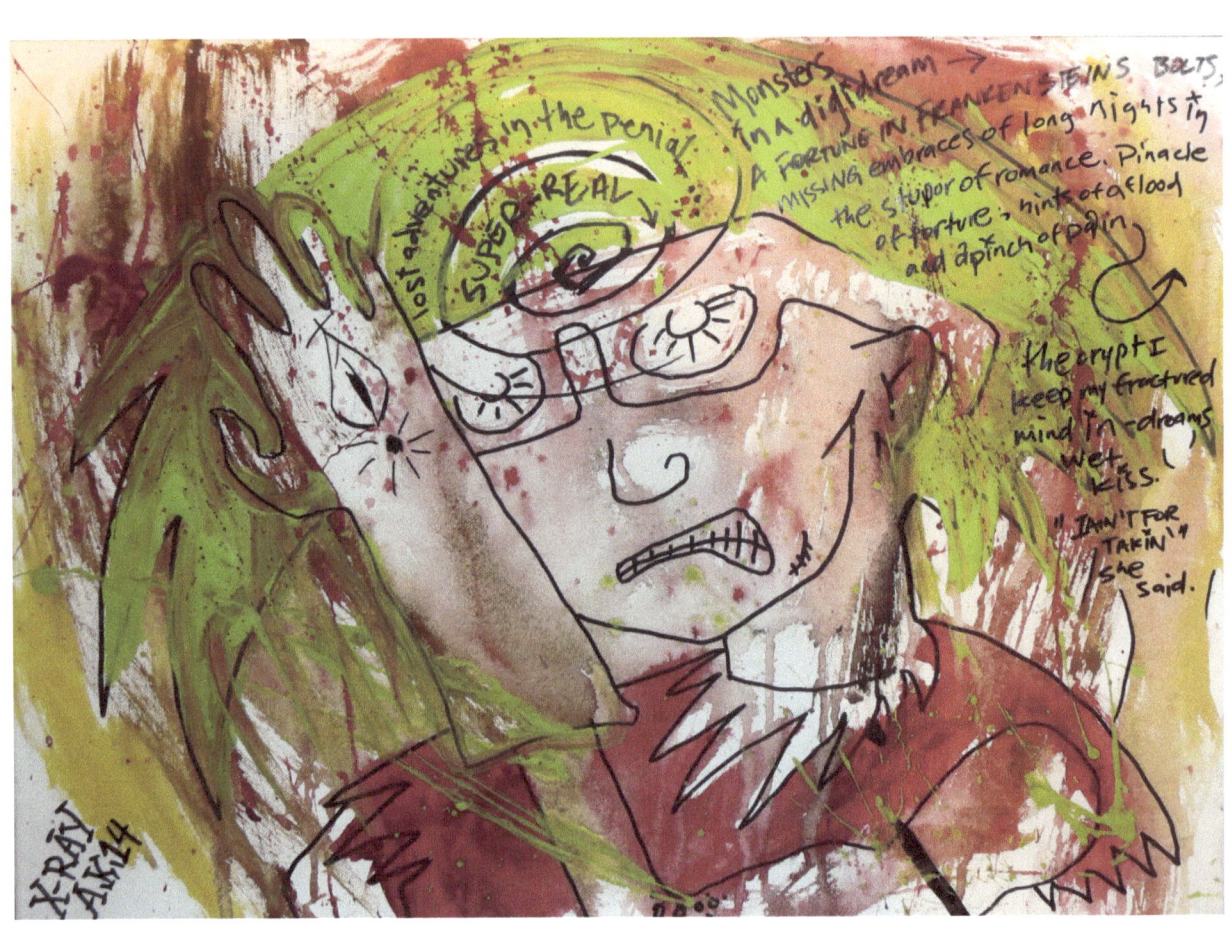

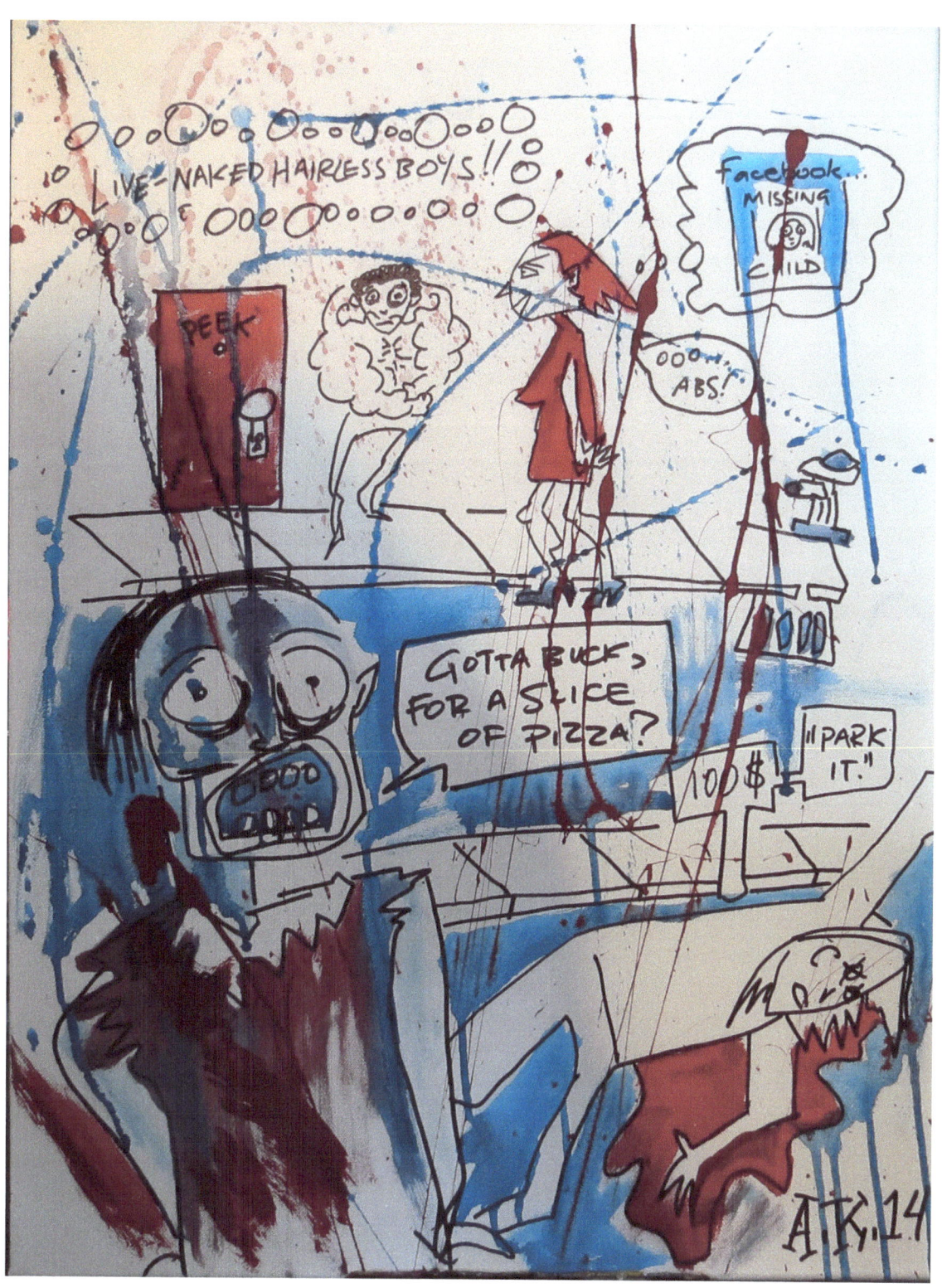

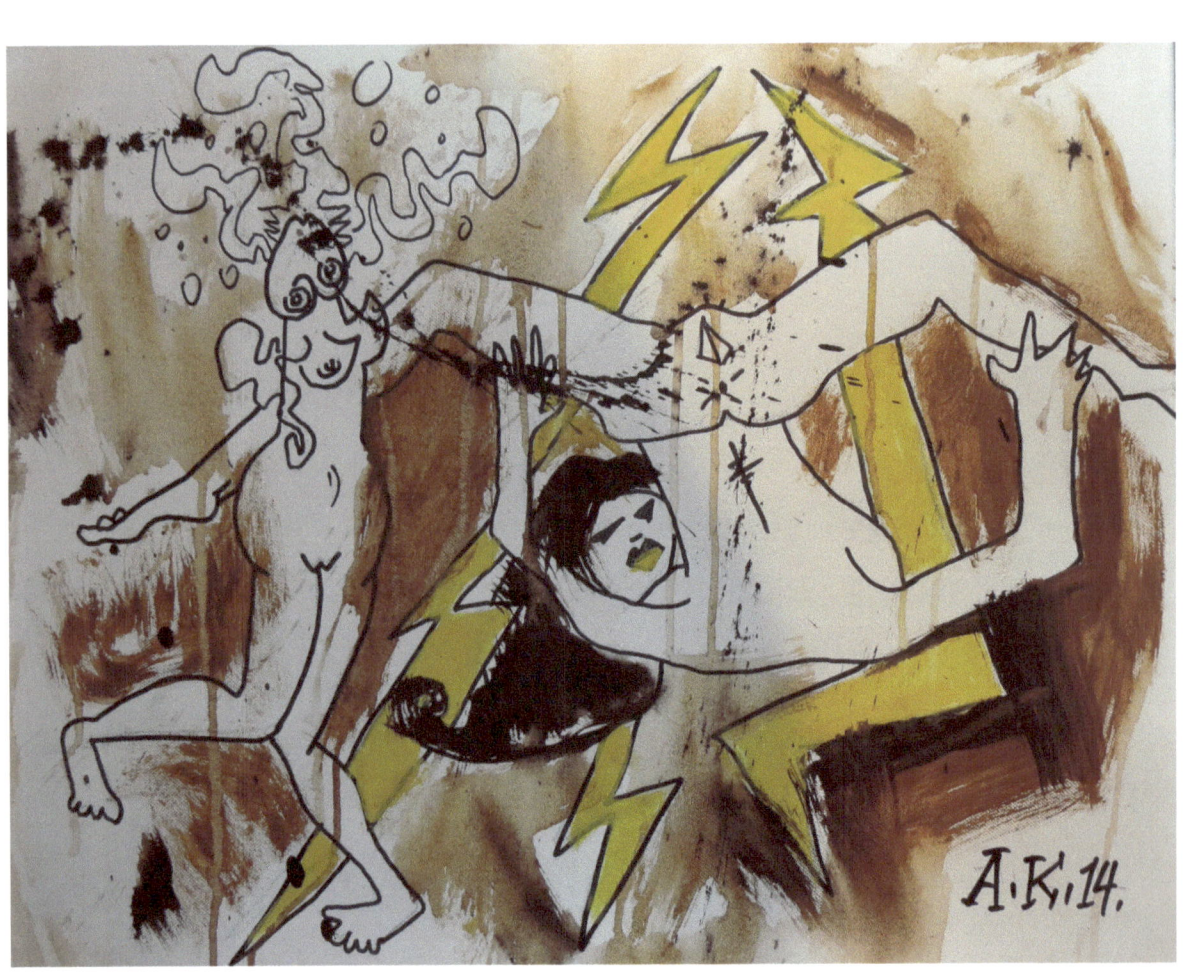

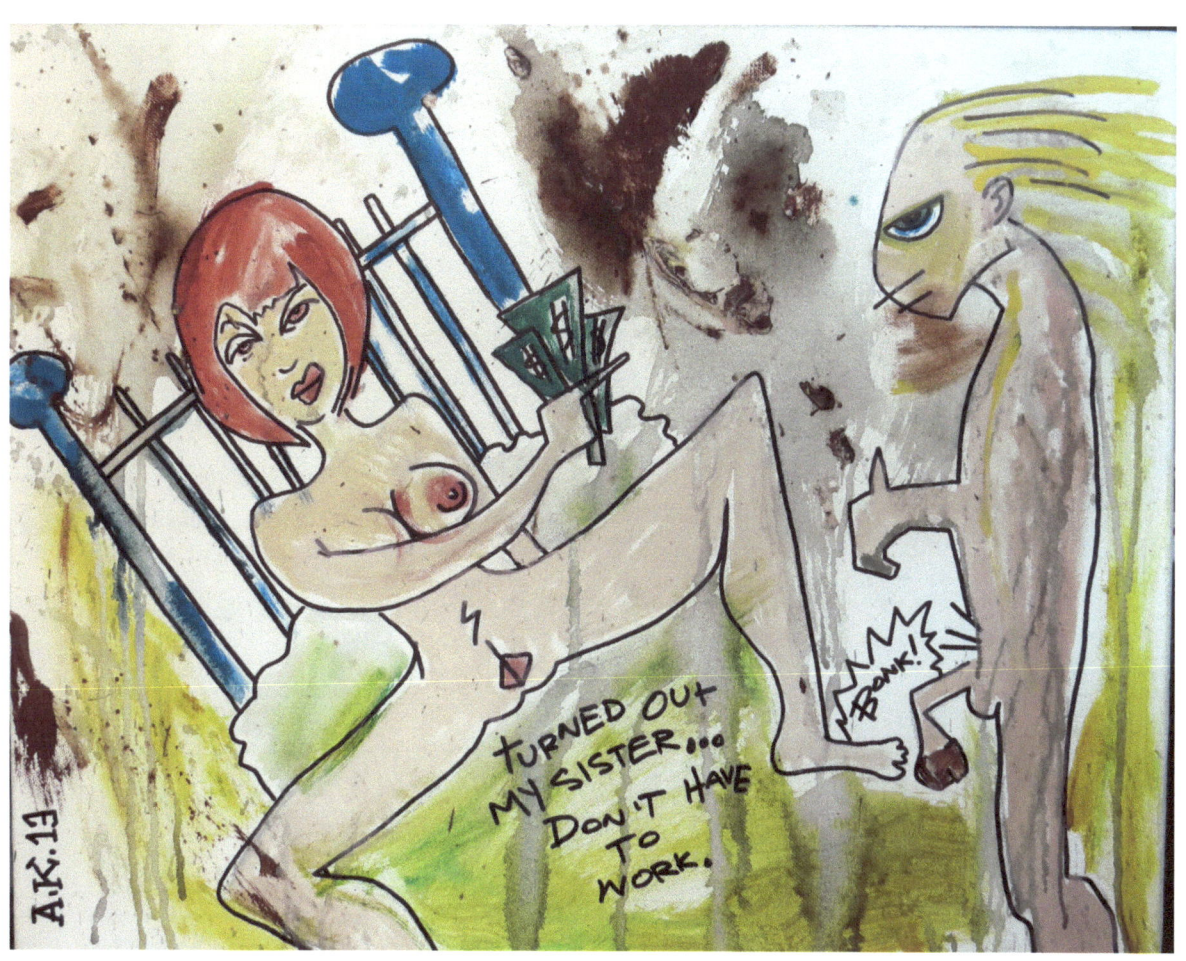

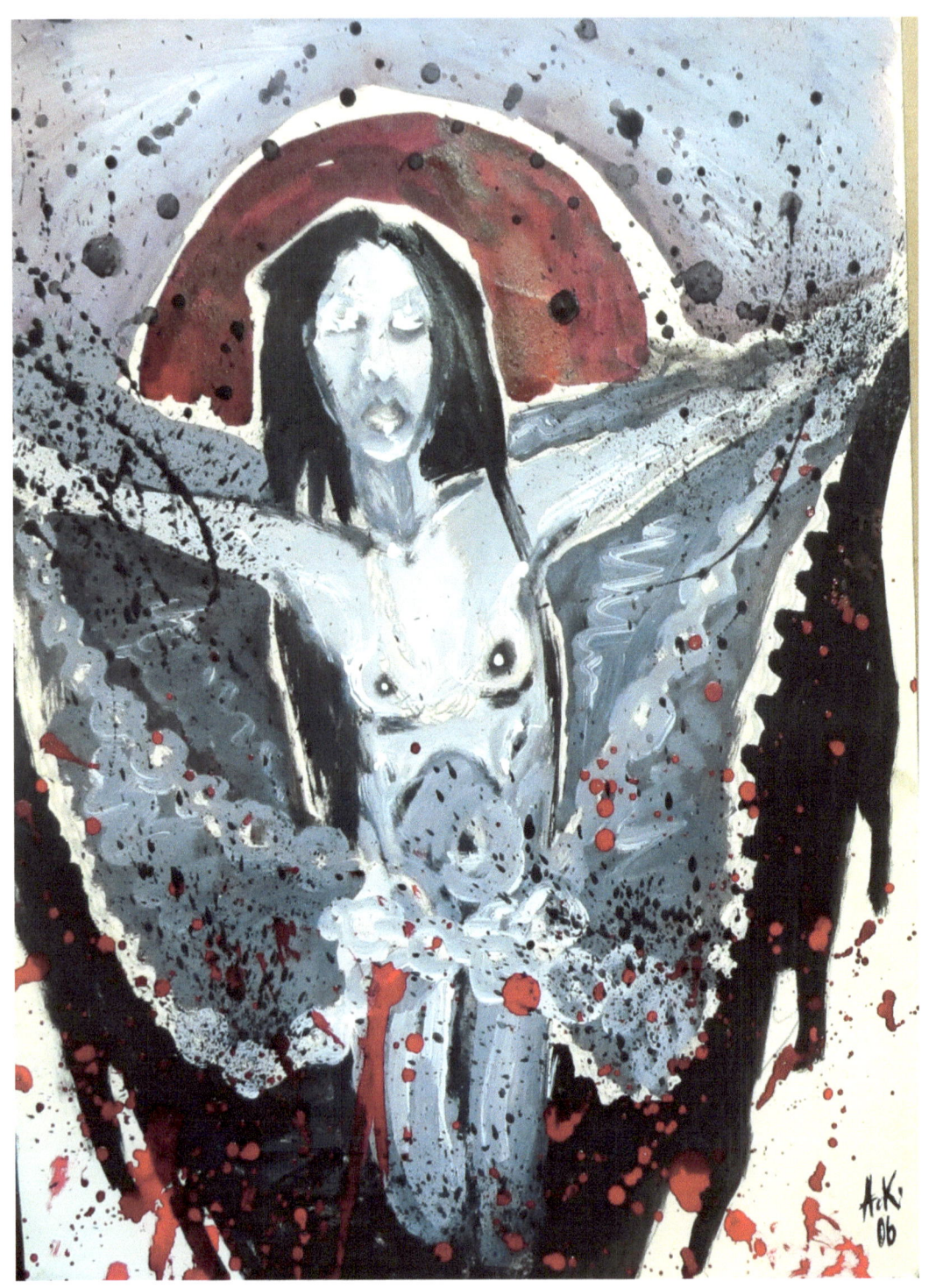

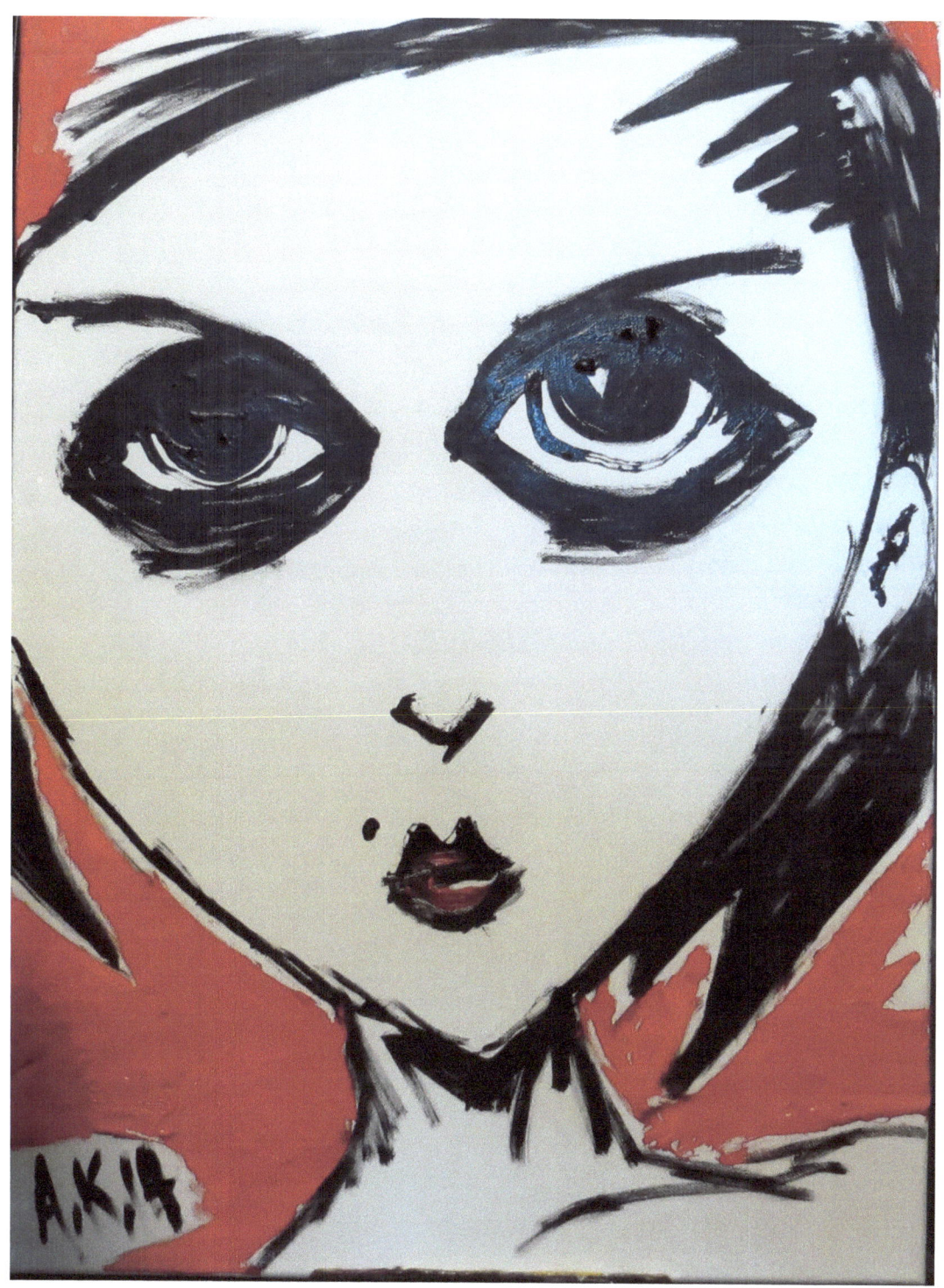

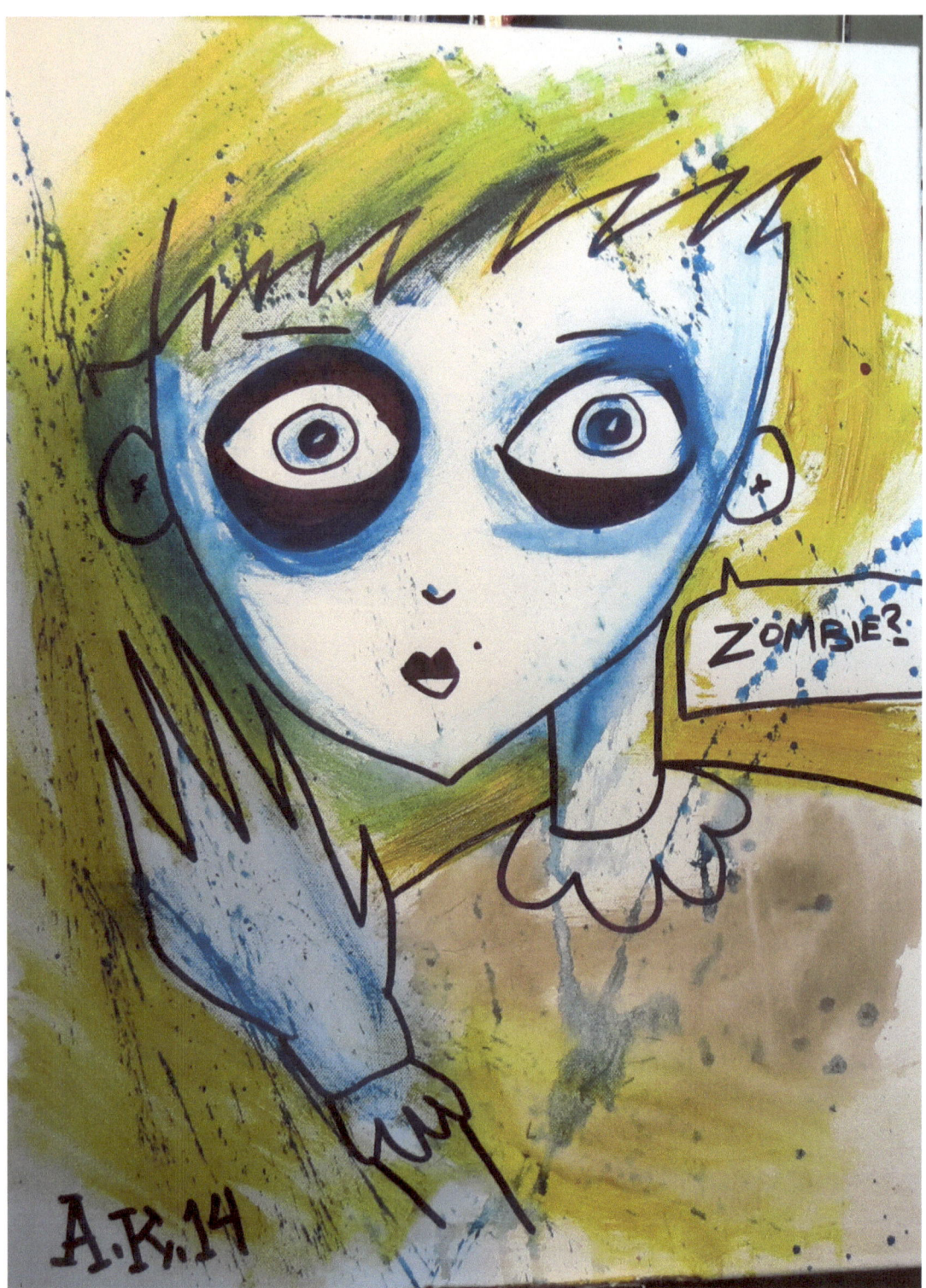

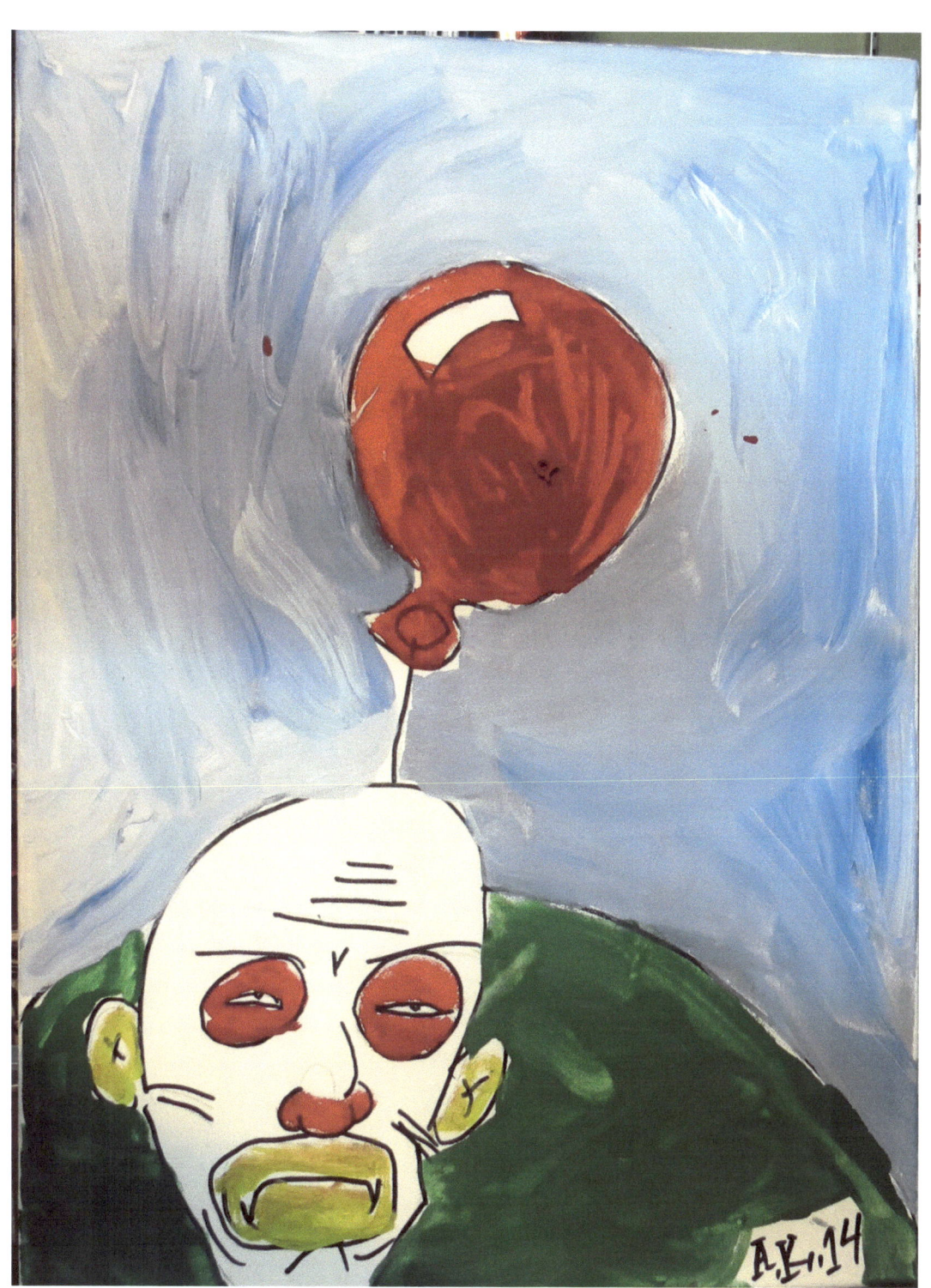

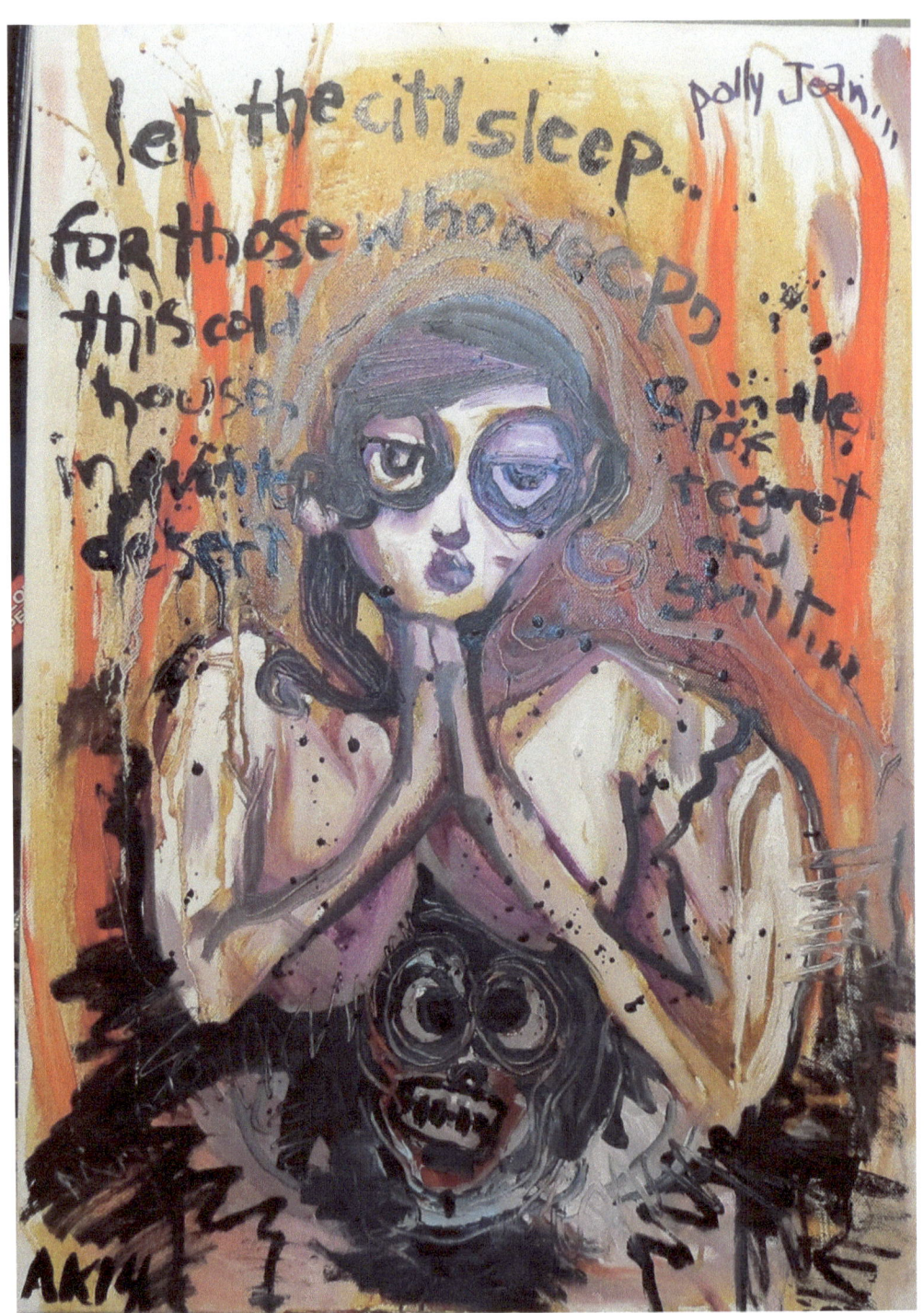

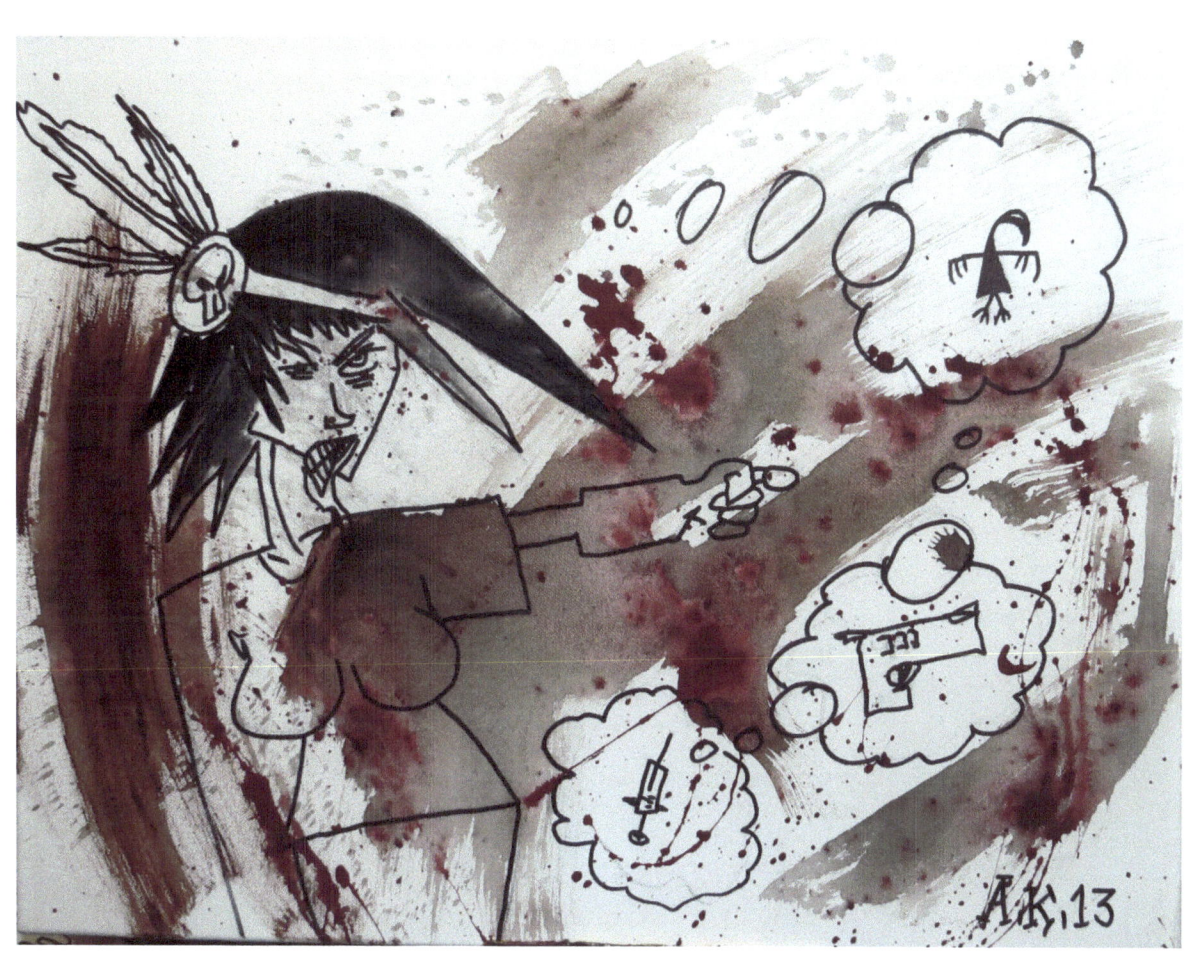

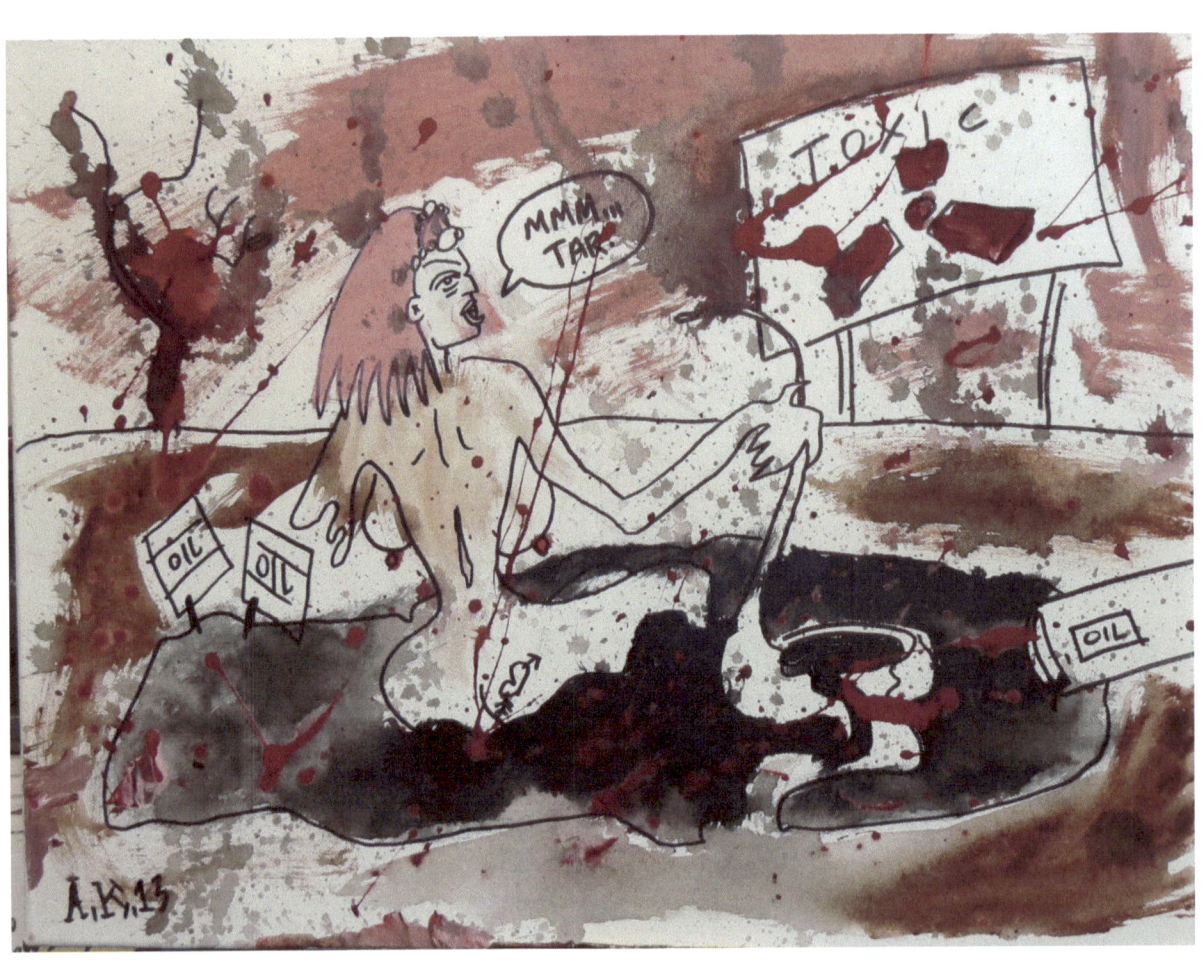

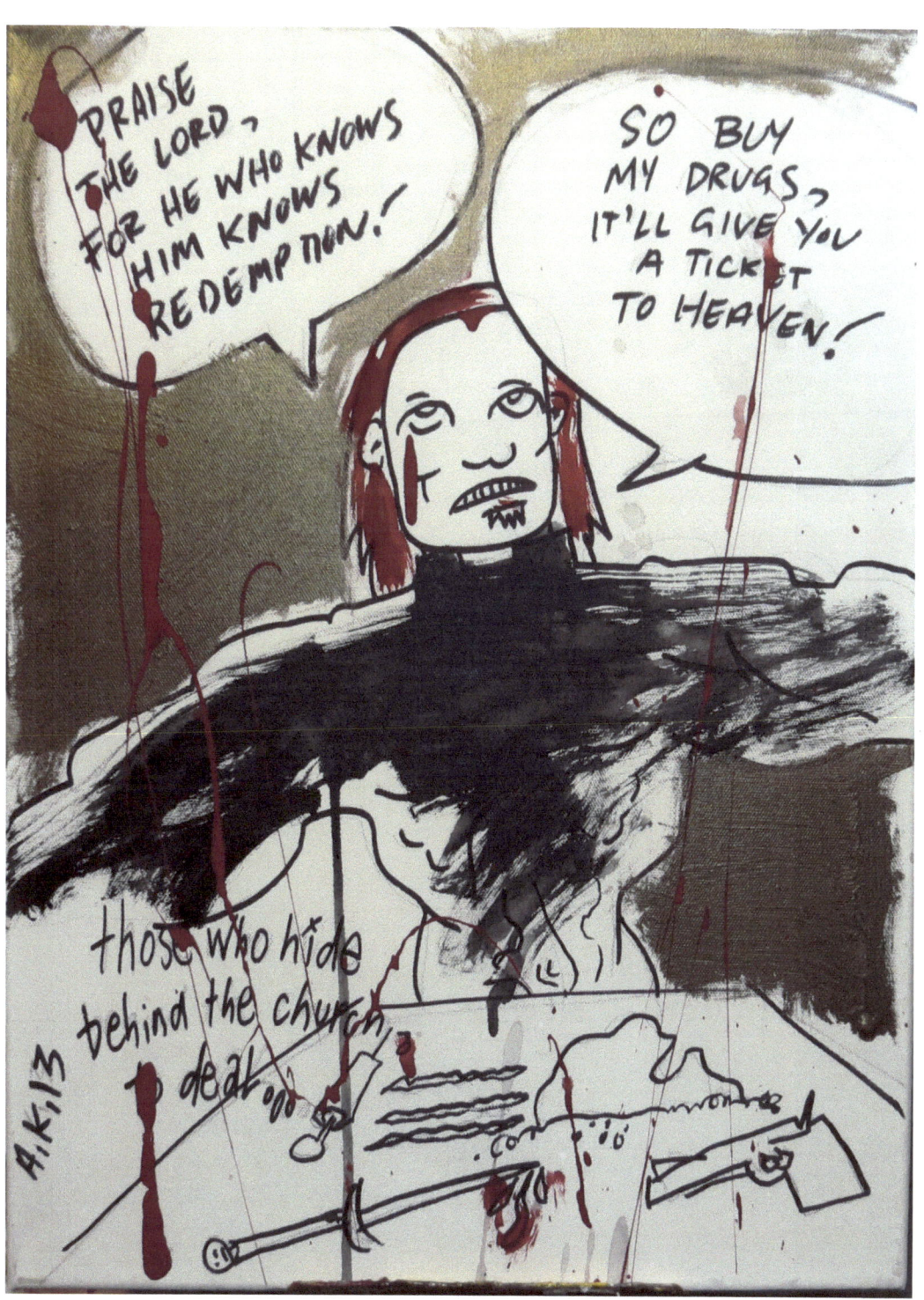

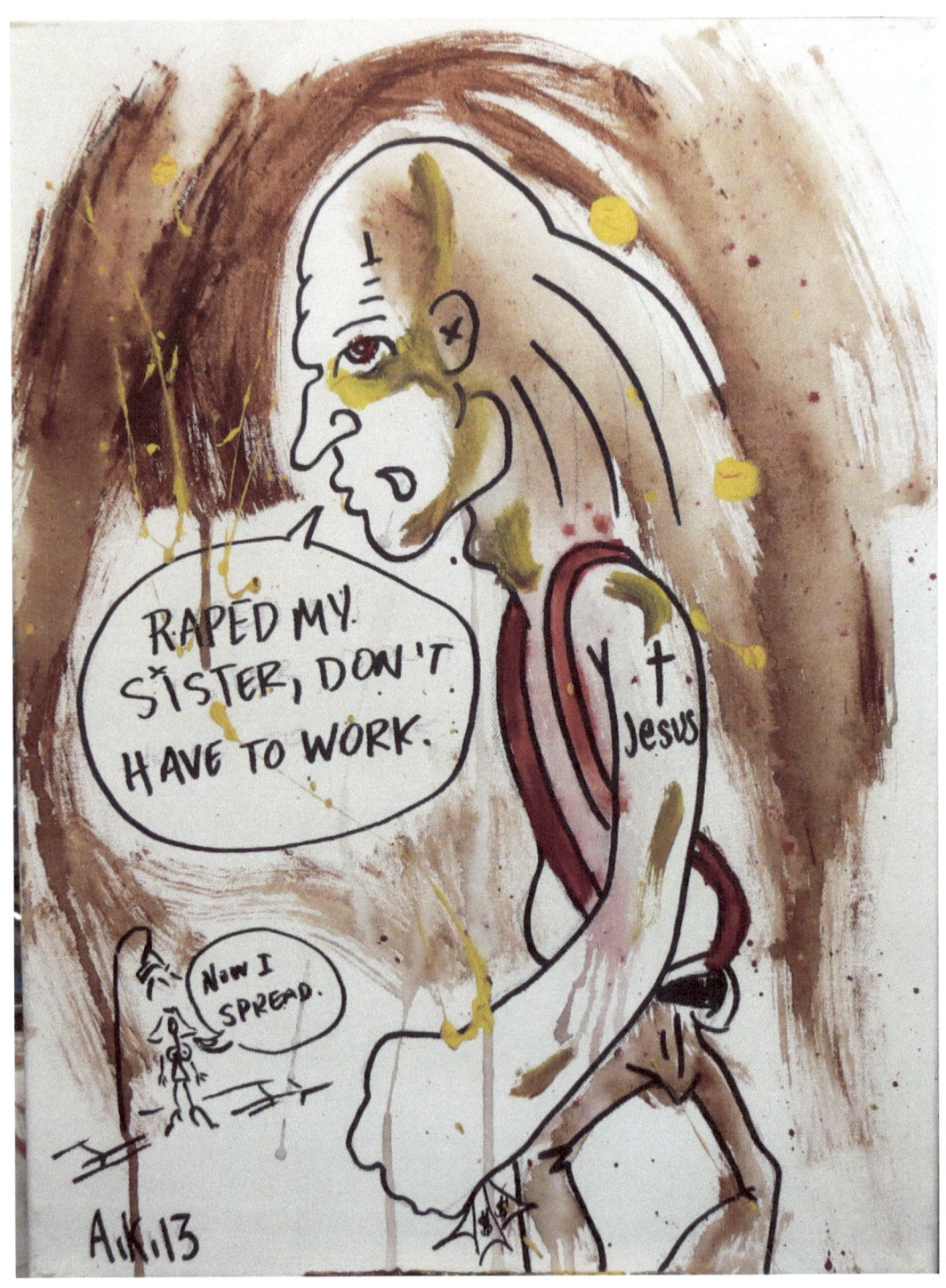

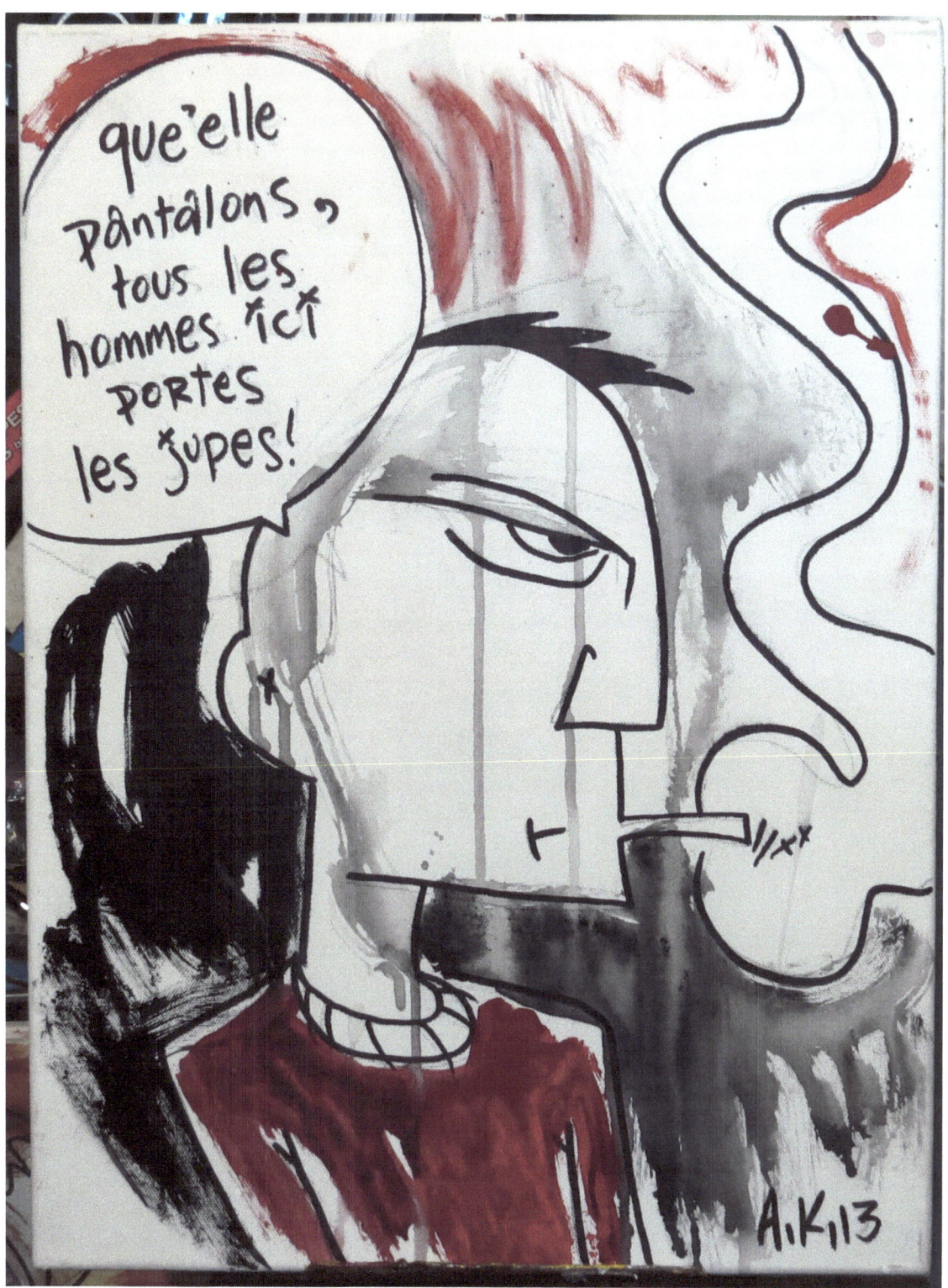

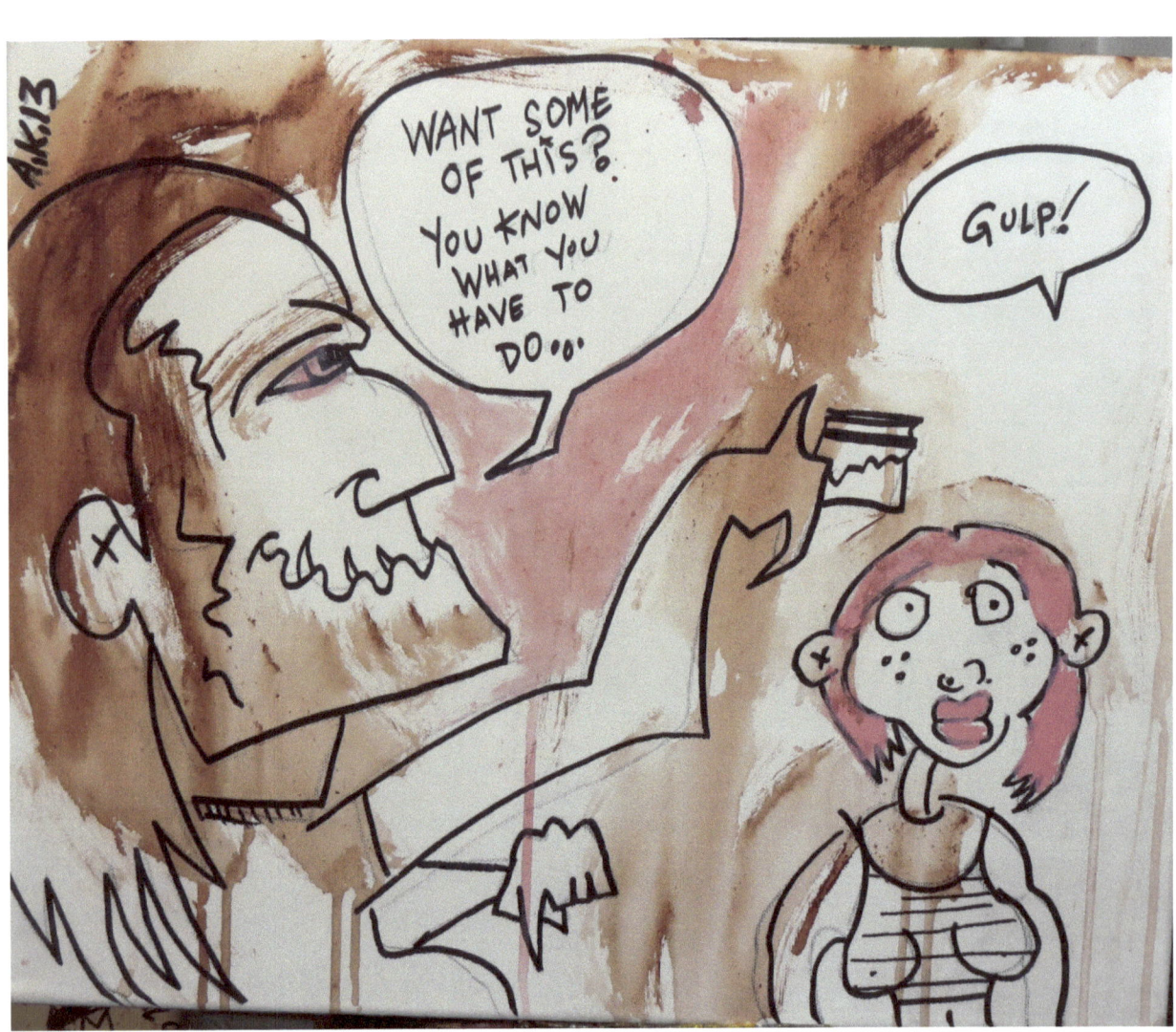

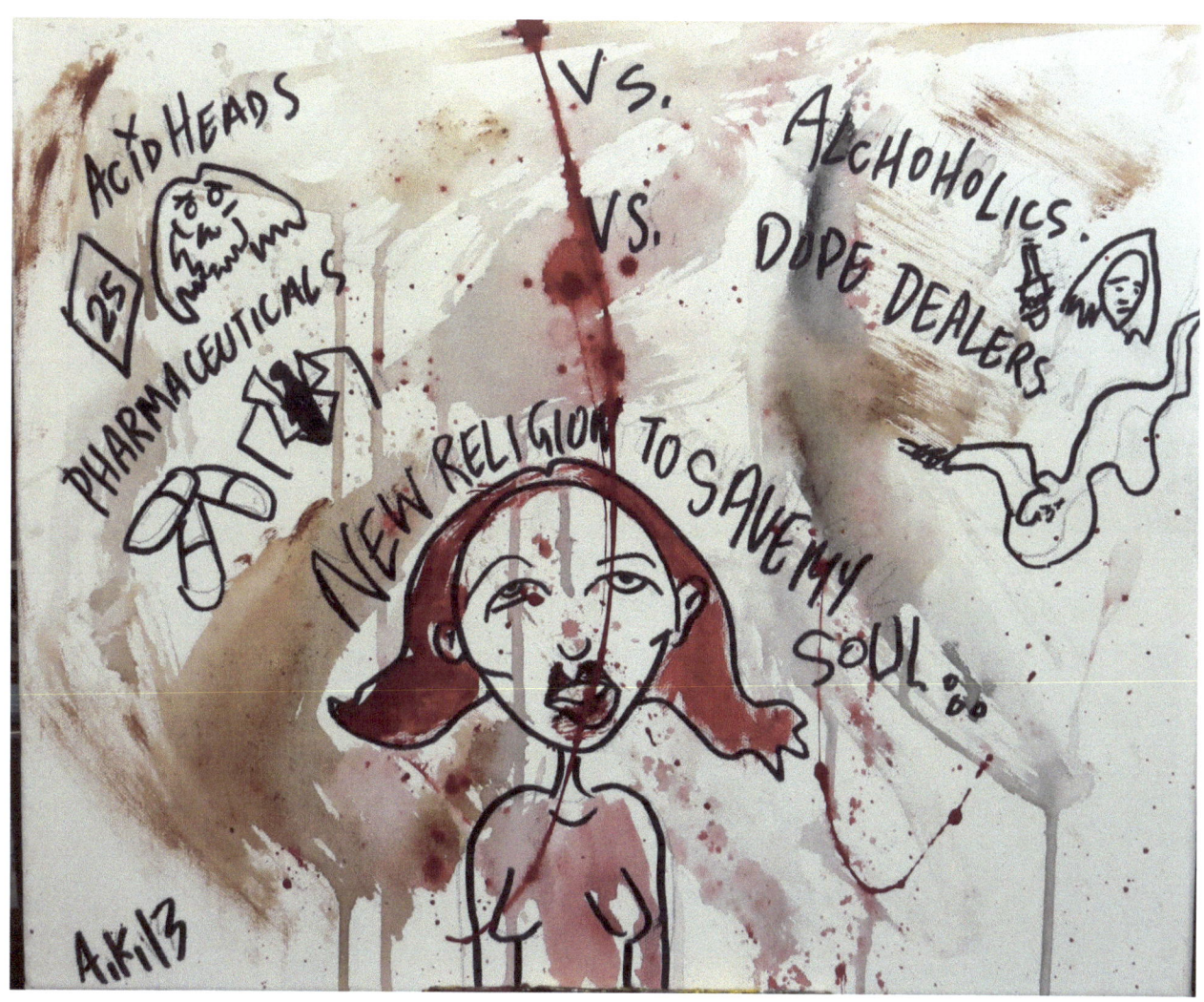

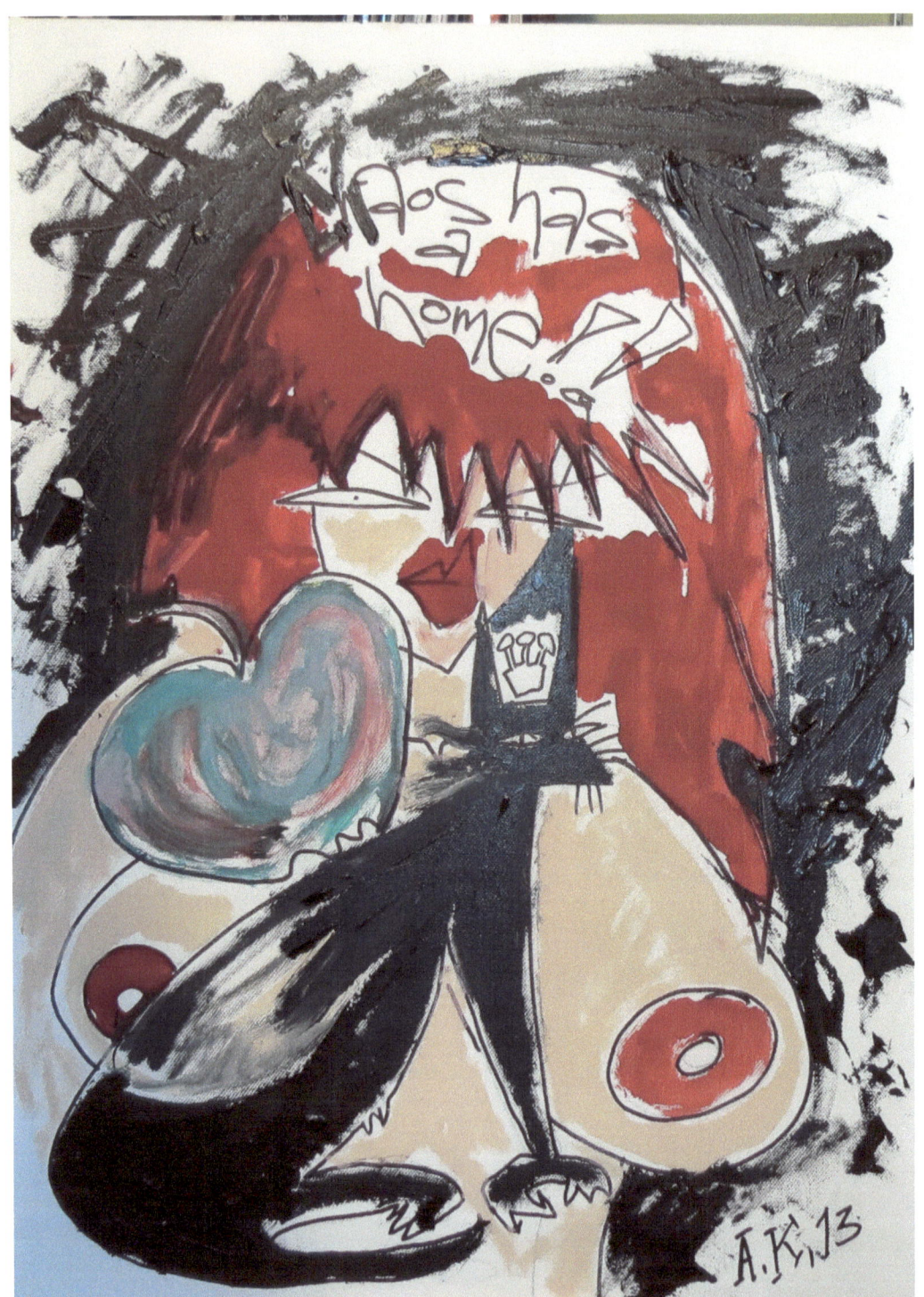

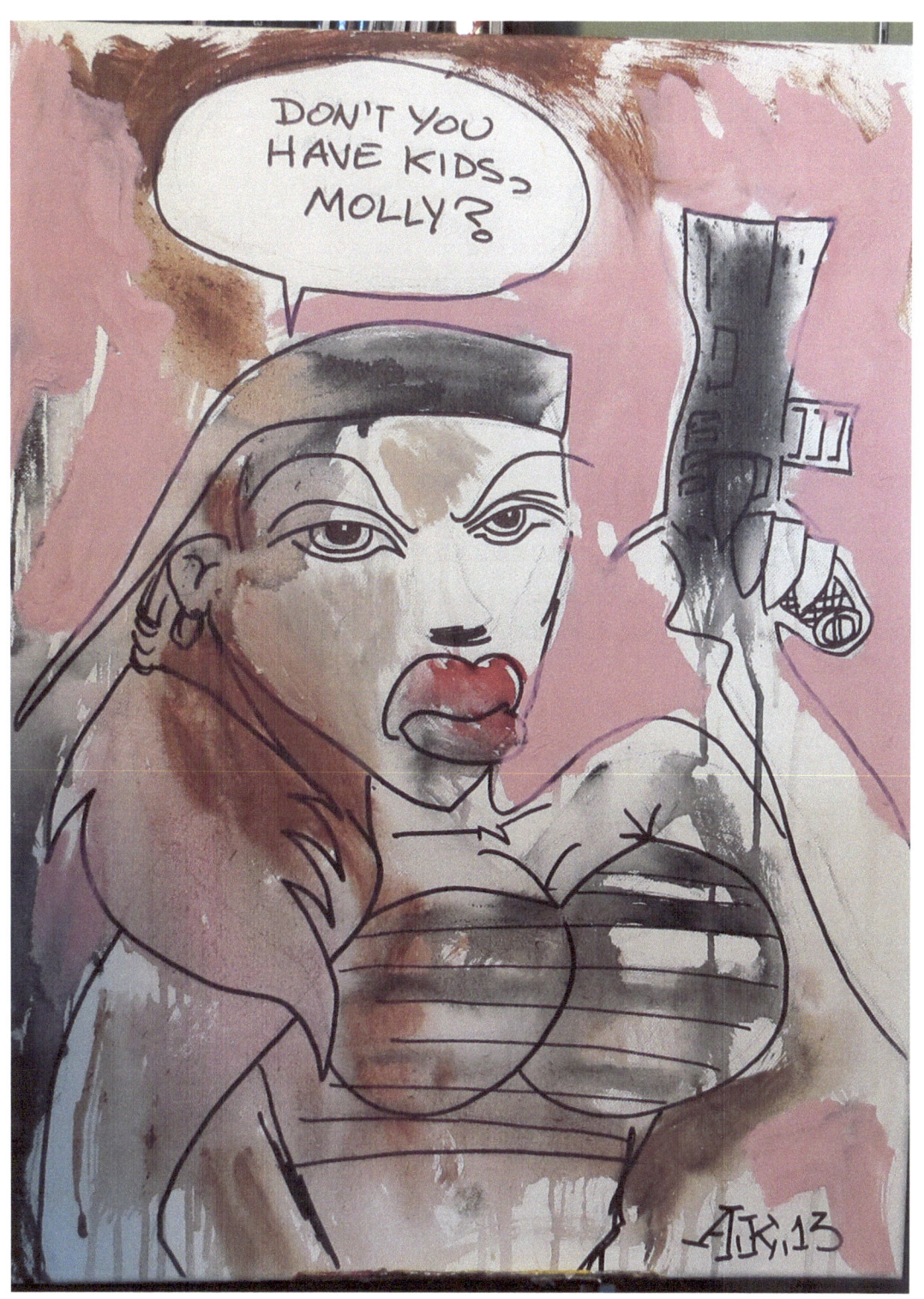

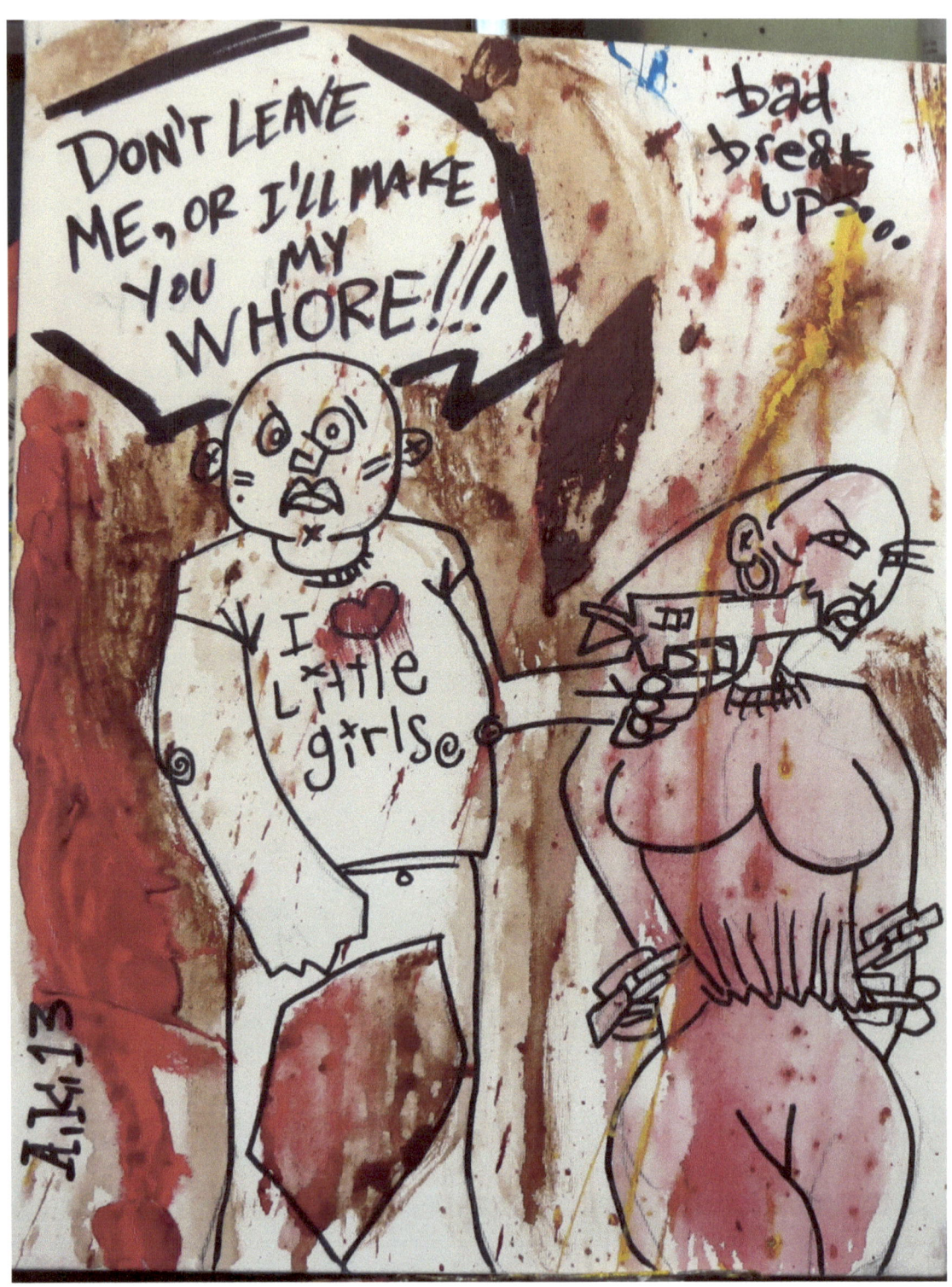

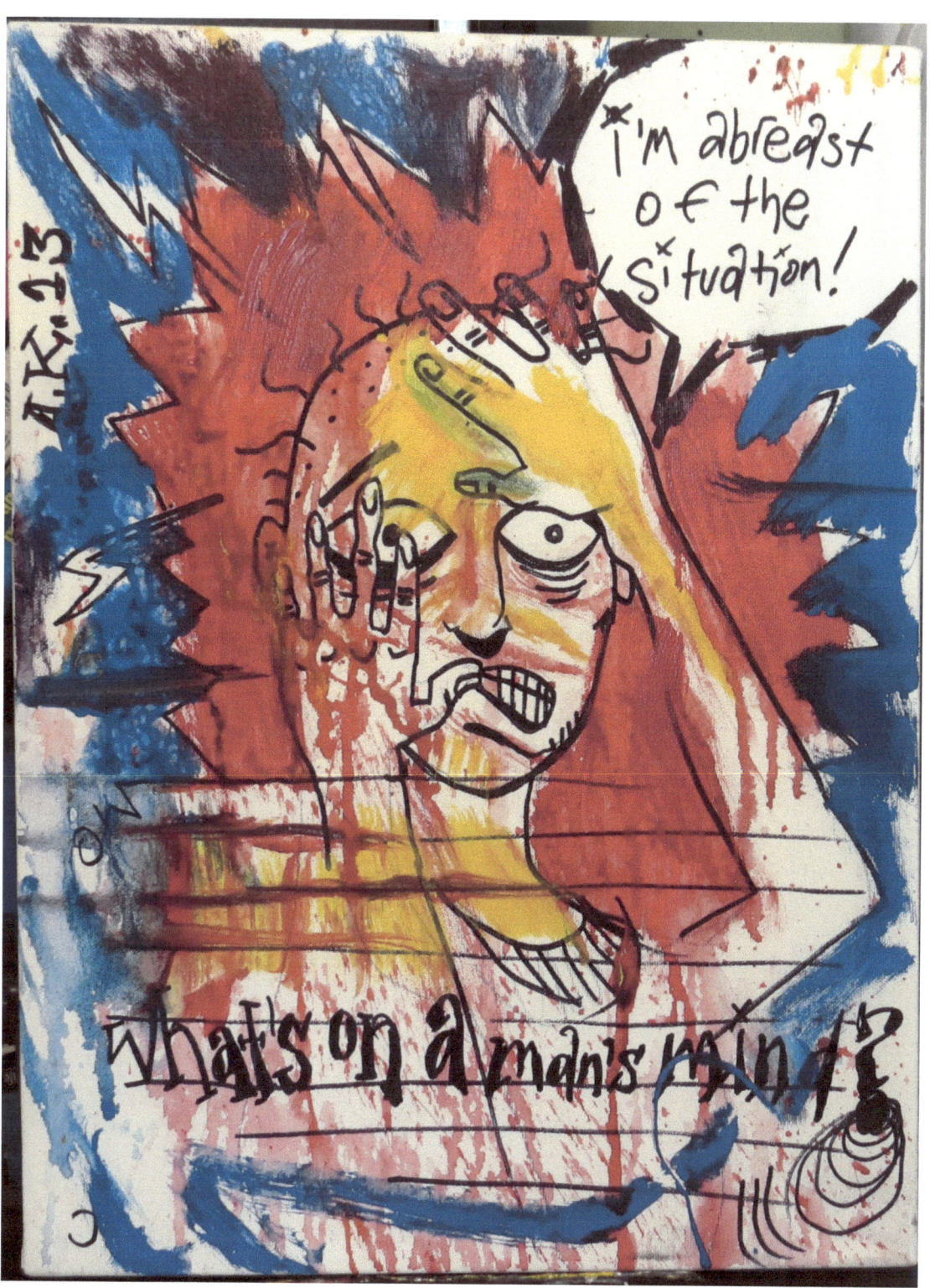

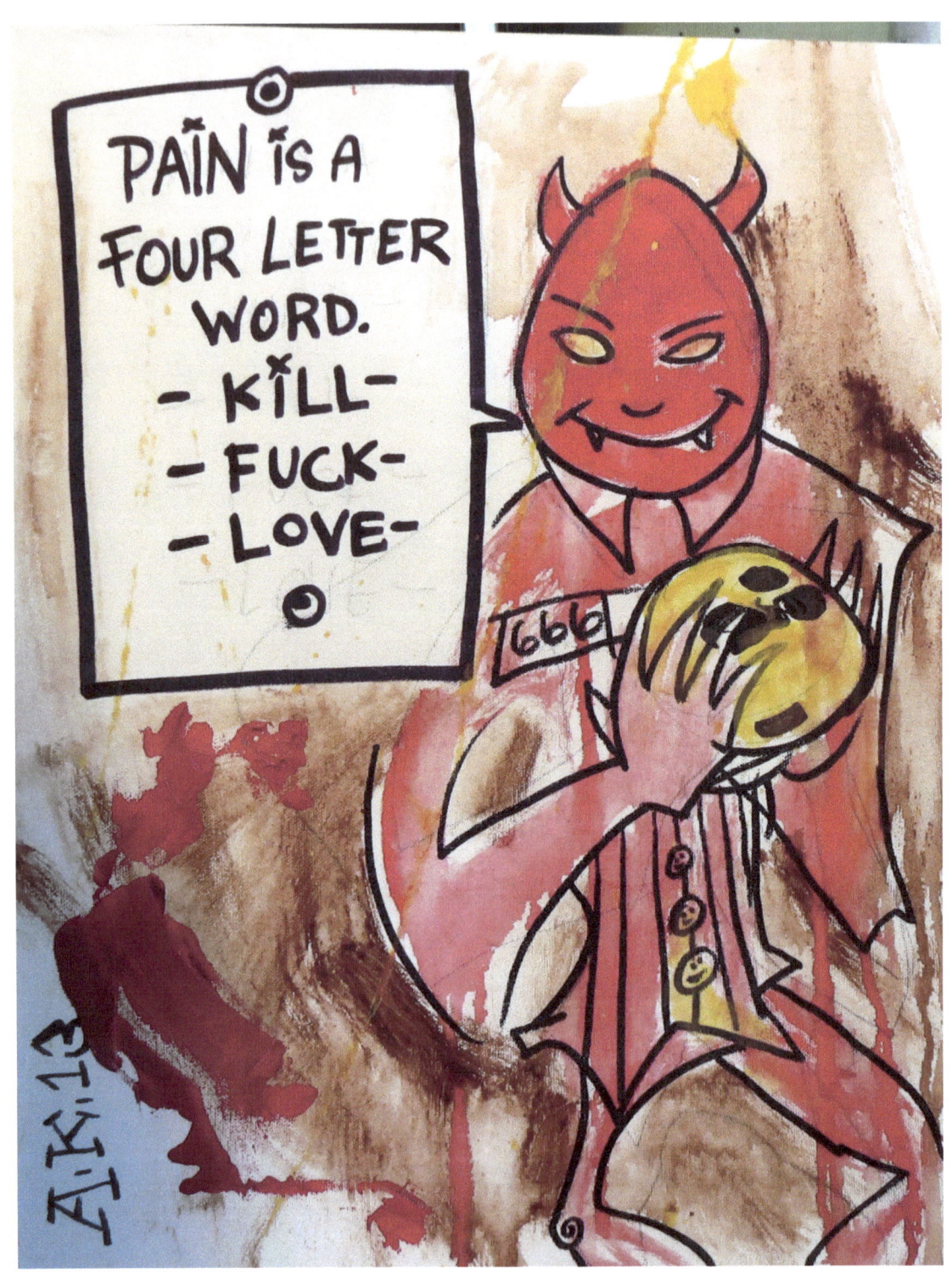

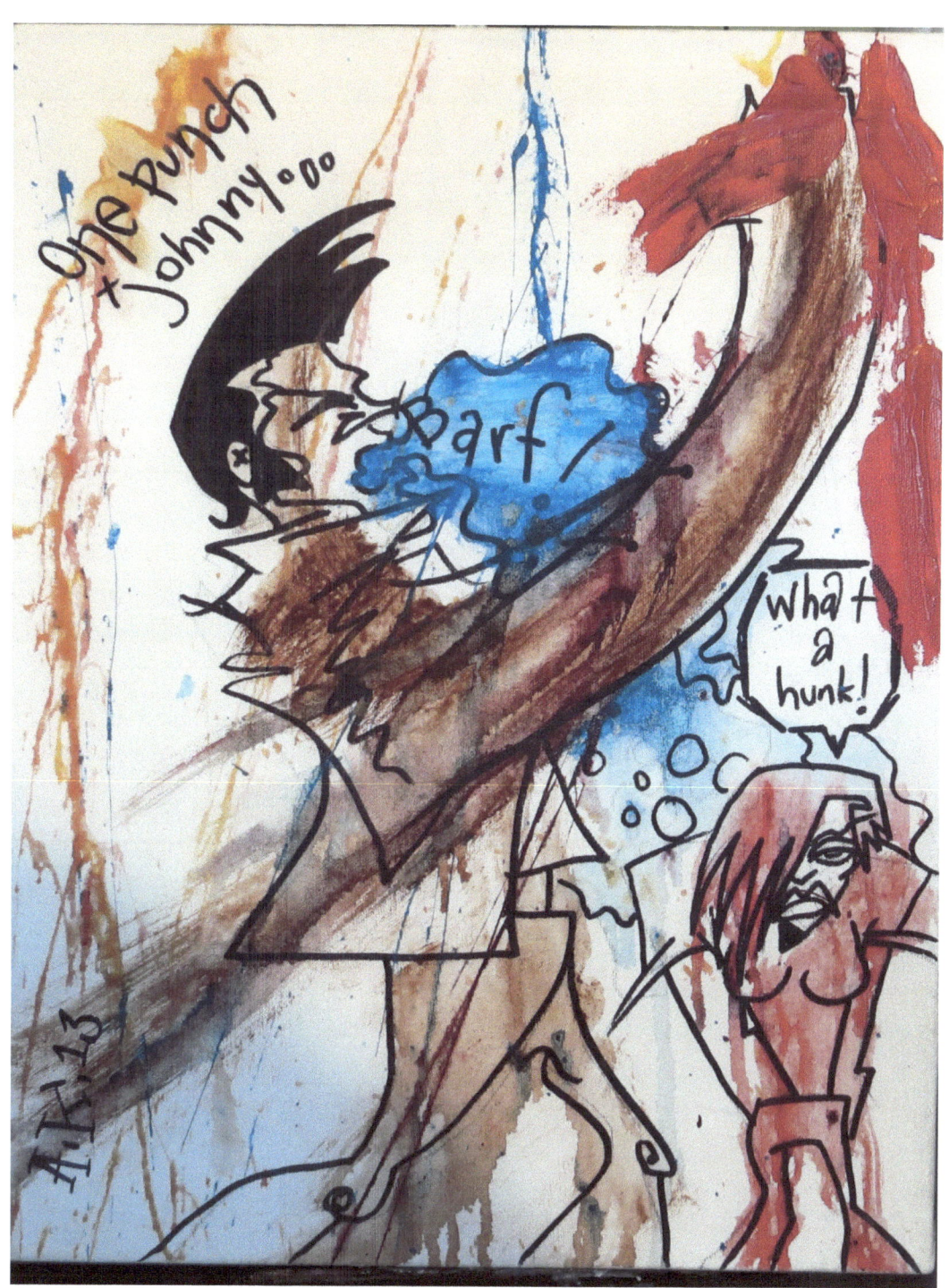

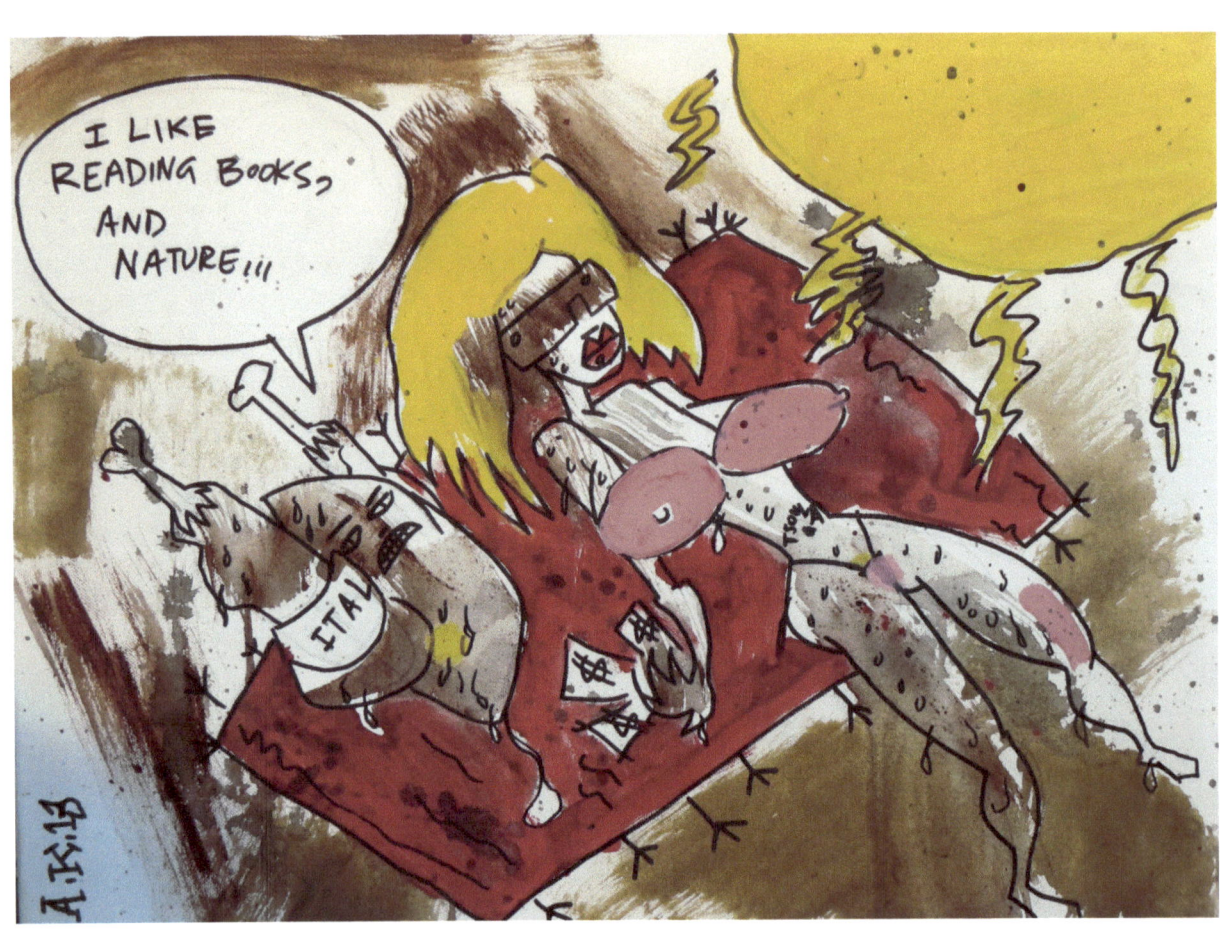

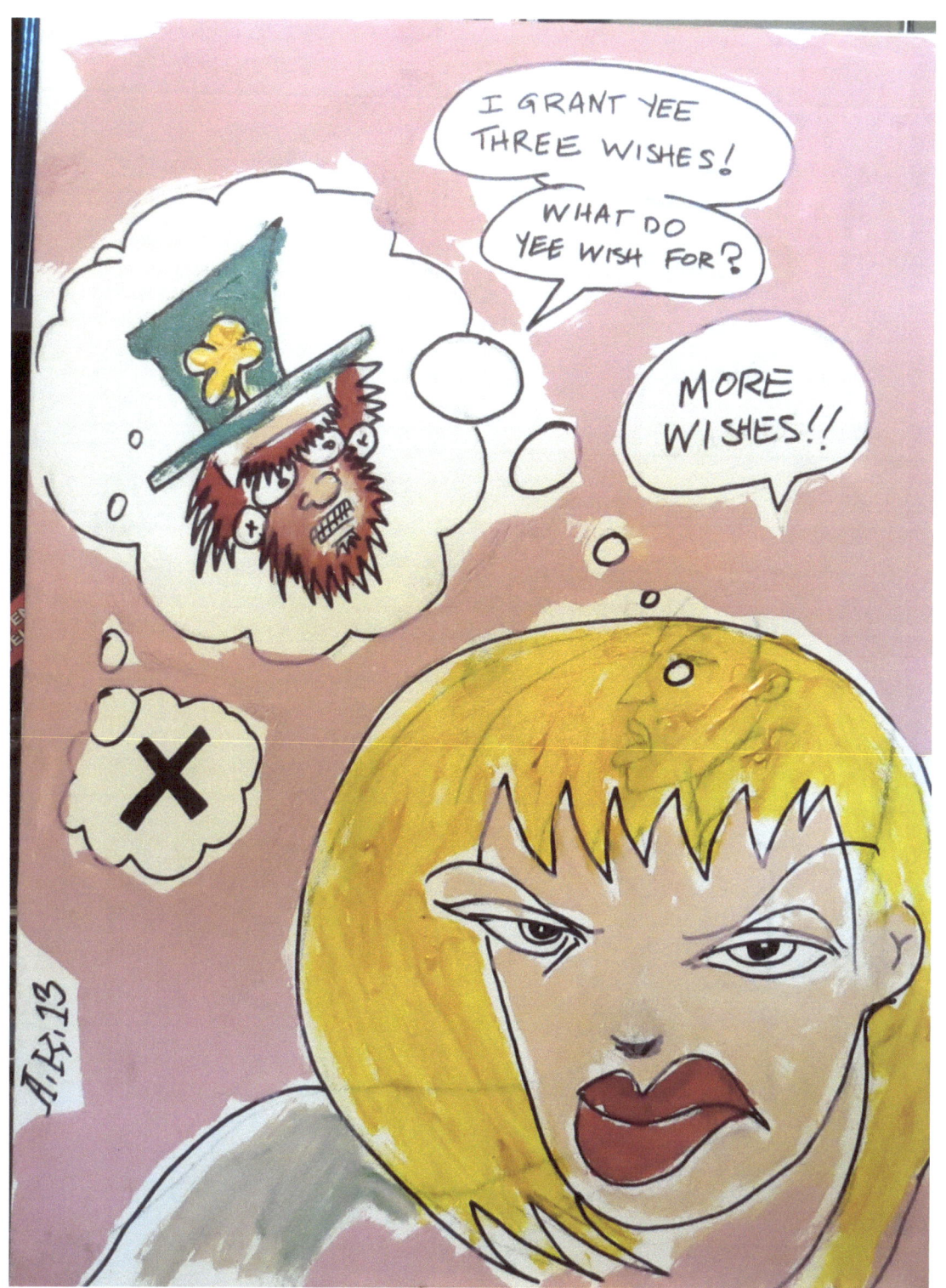

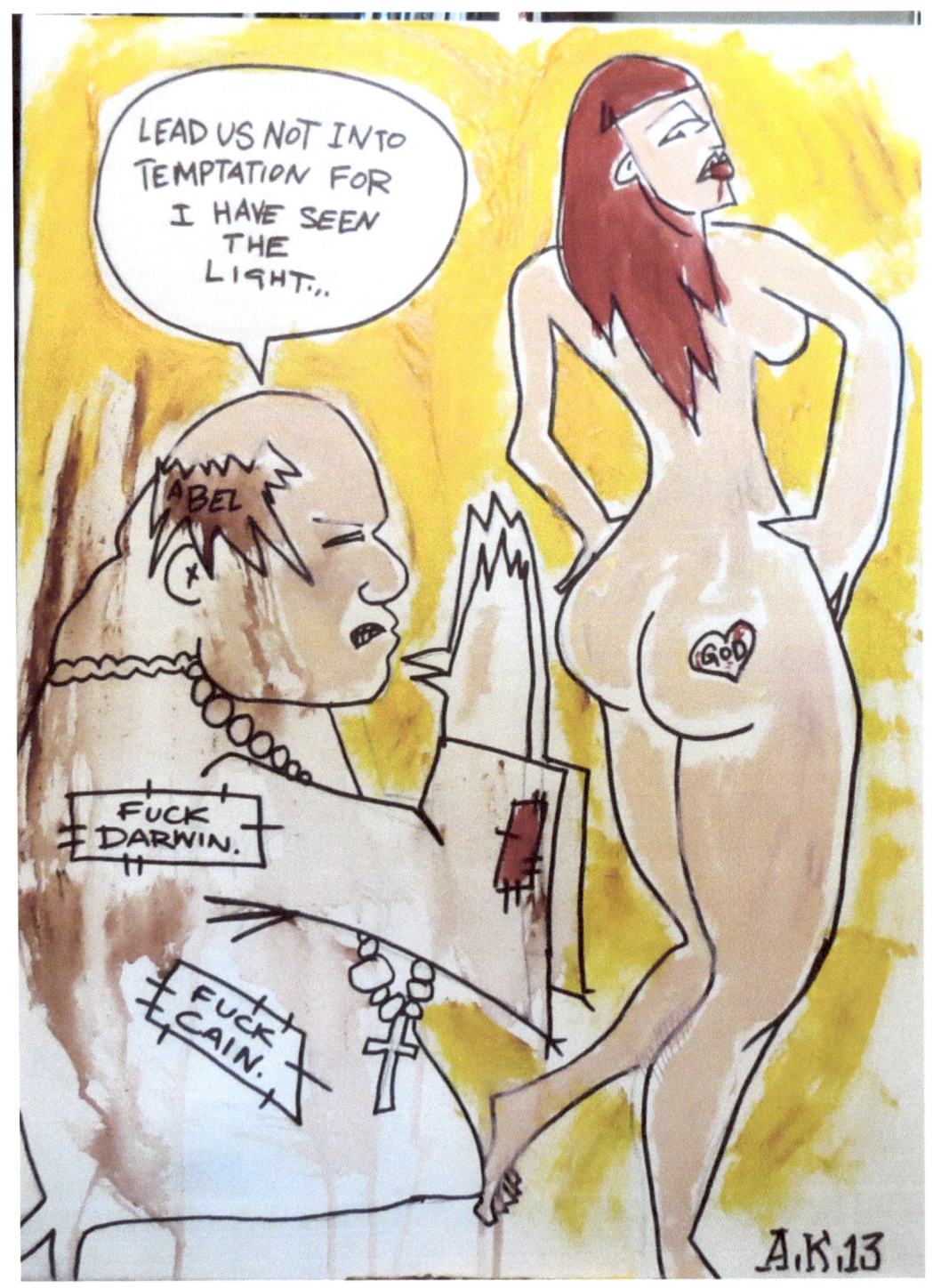

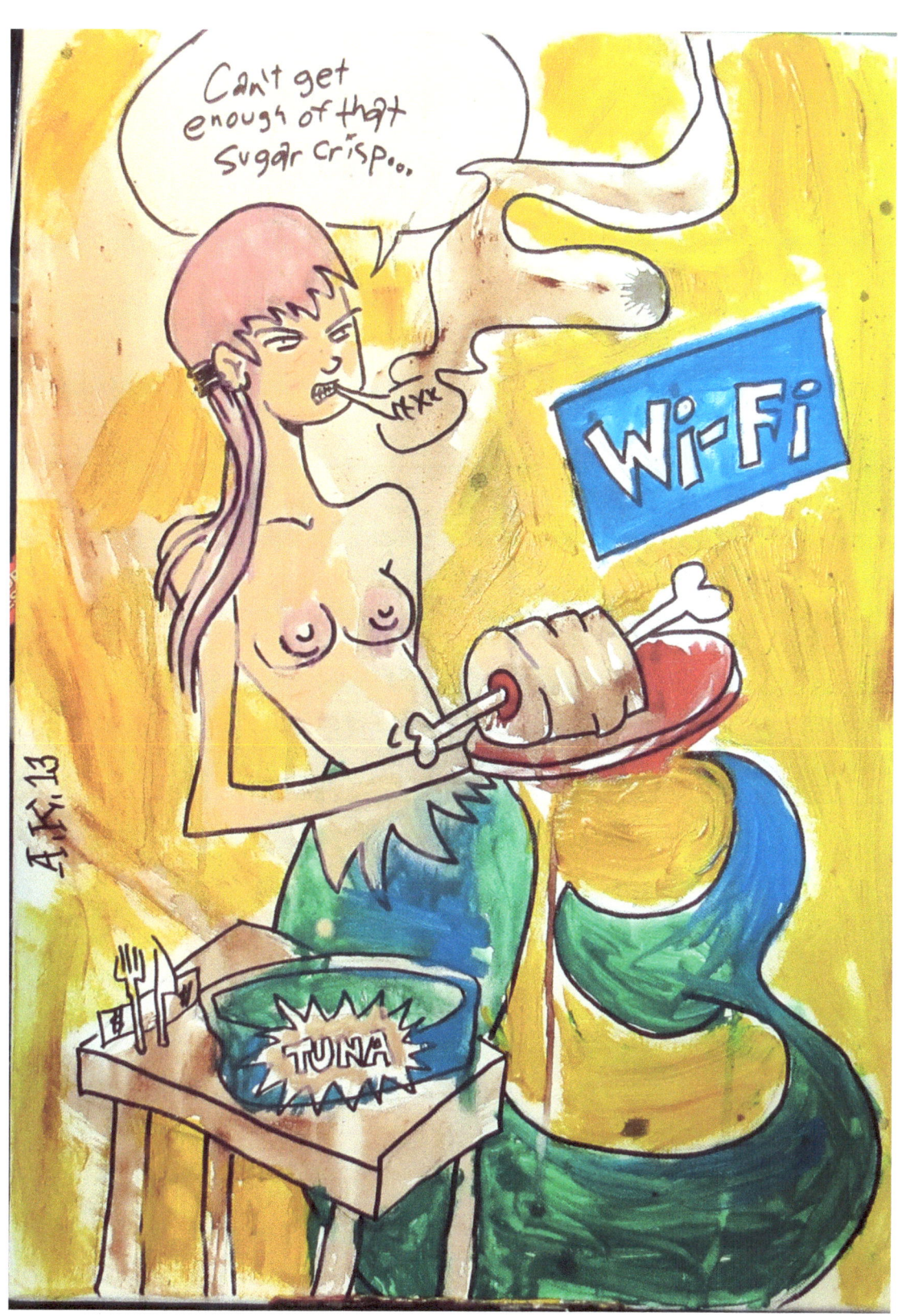

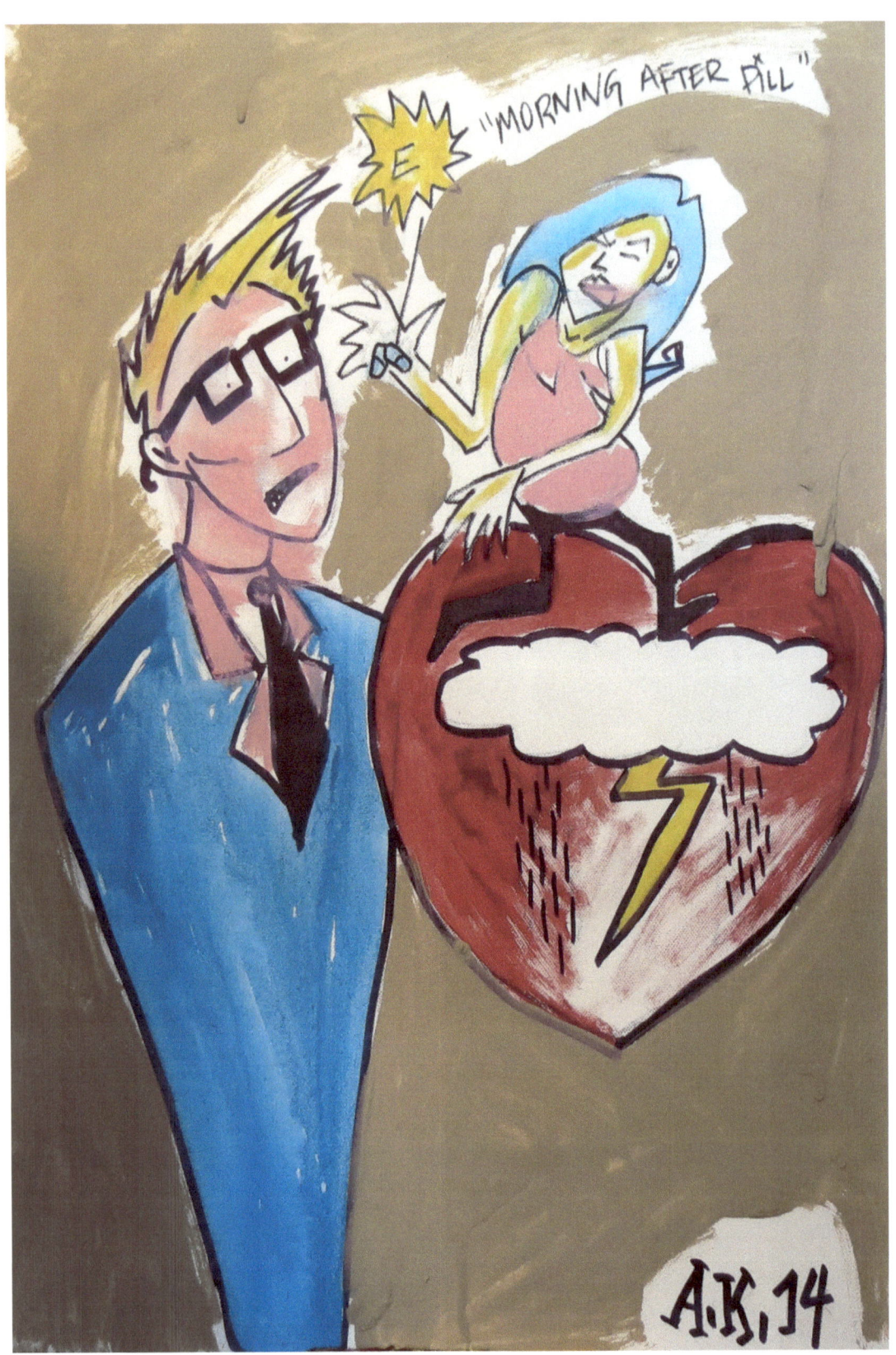

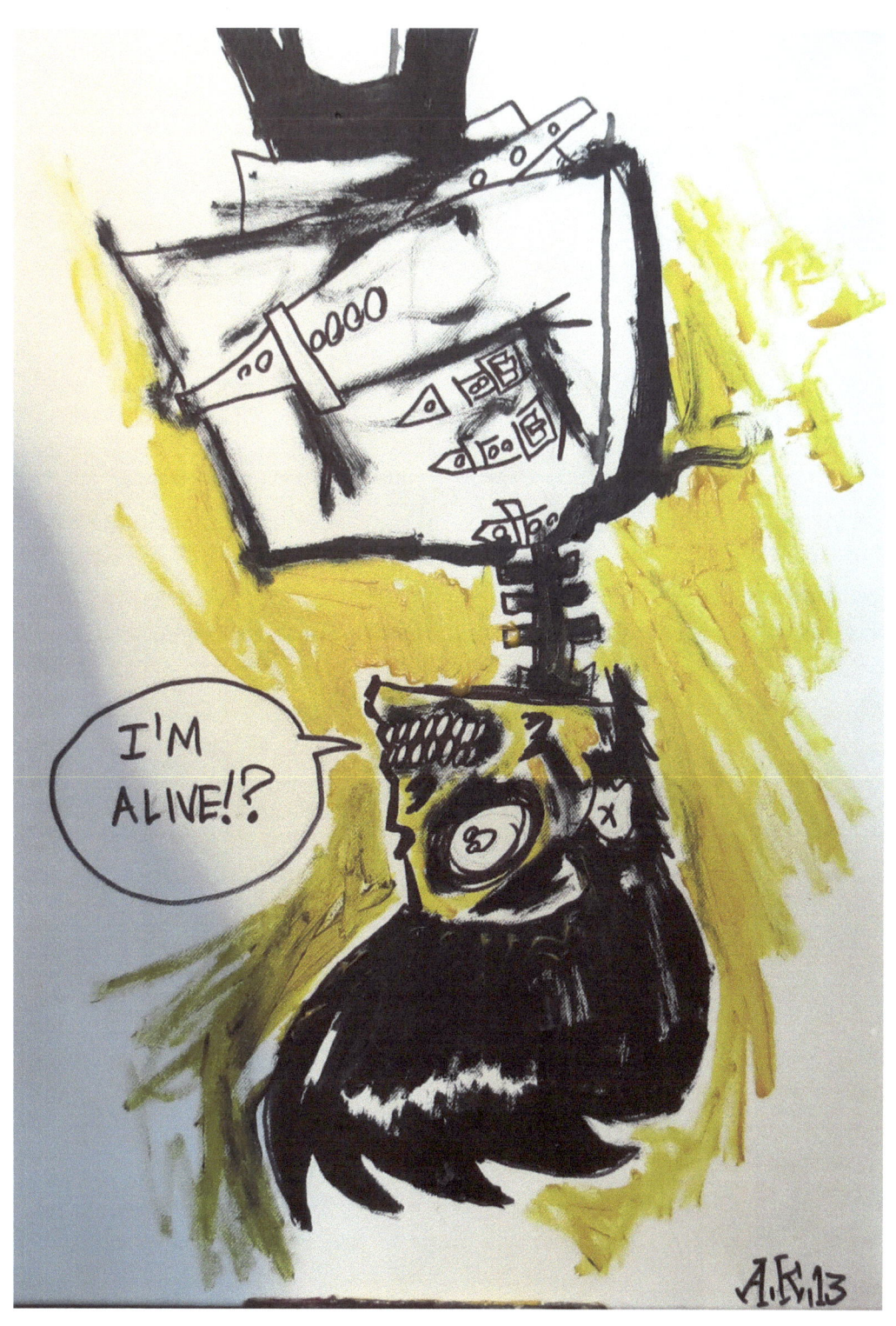

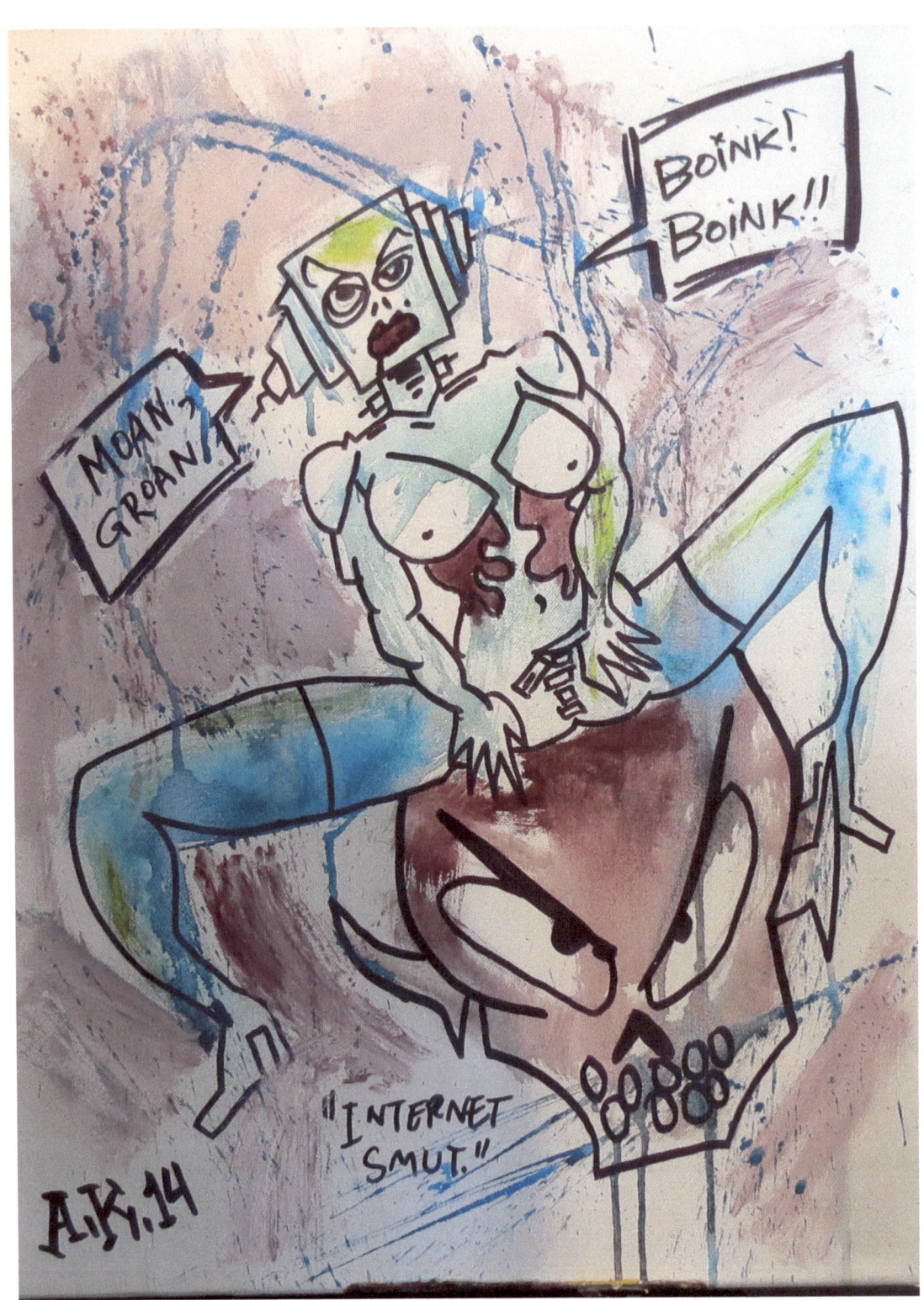

"When The Sun Meets the Earth"   Toly A.K. 2014

"When The Sun Melts the Earth"   Toly A.K. 2014-04-07
I count all of God's creatures on Noah's Arc for the coming flood,
one male Kangaroo, one female.
That the Captain Kangaroo and the Skipper and Gilligan.
Statement or question?
Which is it?
Question a question.
Tune in.
Tune out.
Read about it, the great it!
It's not a Mexican whorehouse.
It is a tomato picked ripe from the vine, ready to stew in a pot,
as the sun beats down on your beach hut in Mexico.
Tap your head and rub your belly.
Lay a quarter down on your elbow. Snap your arm back and catch it
in your fist.
Can you see your third invisible finger when you hold your two in-
dex fingers in front of your eyes, pointing toward one another?
Each human has eleven fingers unless they weren't born with each
finger.
Five on each hand, and the eleventh that floats in space.
That finger makes you do evil things.
Yesterday ...was better and around one a.m.
Pumping steel, in florescent gym shorts and sporting a tribal tattoo not your thing? Allow me to introduce you to your new you.
Paulie Shores diet book, void of Bengal Hollywood (of course),
this new you will promote and incite Magnavox pupil dilation, and
retinal stimulation, as you tattoo your brain, a nice new glowing
skull.
Uncle Papa Jimmy, fresh from the fire of psychedelic break and en-
ter sits in a ravine next to buildings in South Africa waiting for
the Mongoose to fly so he can shoot it down and feast like the an-
cients.

Can you cut yourself in cathartic revelation so you might bleed a shroud of Turin for it is foretold only the blood of an urban whore can animate the corpse of resurrection.

I typically don't like the over the top stuff, I'm just so disgusted with myself and humanity I can't help it.

This book is phoney.

A dog will bite you in the face for Christmas.

A bunch of zits a stack of pills to pay your bills.

A priest came to the house today, he's like "we need to talk" not sure if he's aware Christian re-programming is illegal in Quebec.

The cheapest way to kill someone is by running them over with a car.

Another, which I'm sure is being deliberated upon is getting a trigger happy rookie I suppose, it's kind of like building your house with hard wood ceilings.

For the most part these writings are a vendetta for the homeless, as the rich elite push them further into committing crimes through decadent words-pushing them onto the sidewalk from high school.

Personally, hundreds of years from now my mummified corpse will be found by some scholars will deem that I came from strange third world country because of the calluses, broken bones and scars, while still building great copulation oops corporation with the carcasses of their offspring.

Every time you take a hit off a dime bag, and I ain't into the preachy shit but a cop gets trigger happy, a guy in prison dies, a lawyer pays his mortgage and Suzie cream cheese becomes an orphan, thereby making cheaper manual "Mexican" labour out of white, corn fed English and French people.

So, get in your car, drive four blocks to the corner store for beer and get a speeding ticket on the way...

We've capsized Noah's arc and kept your children in cubicles, plump and juicy for the cannibals kiss and shaved off his incisors to cut chunks of meat off pearl white bones.

As for me, I'm being brainwashed into wearing Italian leather shoes in winter, summer, and spring and fall too chicken to get a tattoo and sporting Ed Hardy.

The Pleebs taking out, their stress and sexual frustration in papa roach style on people and their kids is unparallel in our day and age.

I knew an artist who burned all of his work and called it cathartic, why not burns all of his money?

"Wah, wah, wah..."

I guess a hard working immigrant from a third world country, working minimum wage wouldn't get that, but we are living in third world accommodations, left over from world war 2 to house military families, simply because there's no work and easier to grow dope.

A cold chill creeps up my spine and I fall asleep on my mother's kitchen table. In my dream Alice pops her head out of the rabbit hole, laughing and asks if I'm dead.

"You are the light." The voice says over the loudspeaker, waking me up, the kid behind me pokes me in the ribs, the beast is inside you, he says

Like a three headed monster is ait back in my chair.

Something can be said about rotten fruit from the food bank in Montreal, although it tastes like it was sitting in the basement too long and you may find some extra protien in it; it never tasted so sweet.

It wouldn't have been so bad if John Morgan and his band hadn't planned to murder my x-wife and I and successfully planning and murdering my x-girlfriend to break my band up and steal some fans in the 90's.

He probably arranged the accidental death of an Argonaut warrior as well on the way, and mind raped me.

People say shit happens but its bad mojo that governs certain people.

Hard to believe that guy could pull that off. Countless times he scooped up the baroness H off the sidewalk, half drunk, passed out, so I could take her home to her mother, but it happened.

They say, "Let it go", find a love you once knew; how, when they're murder victims?

Fin?

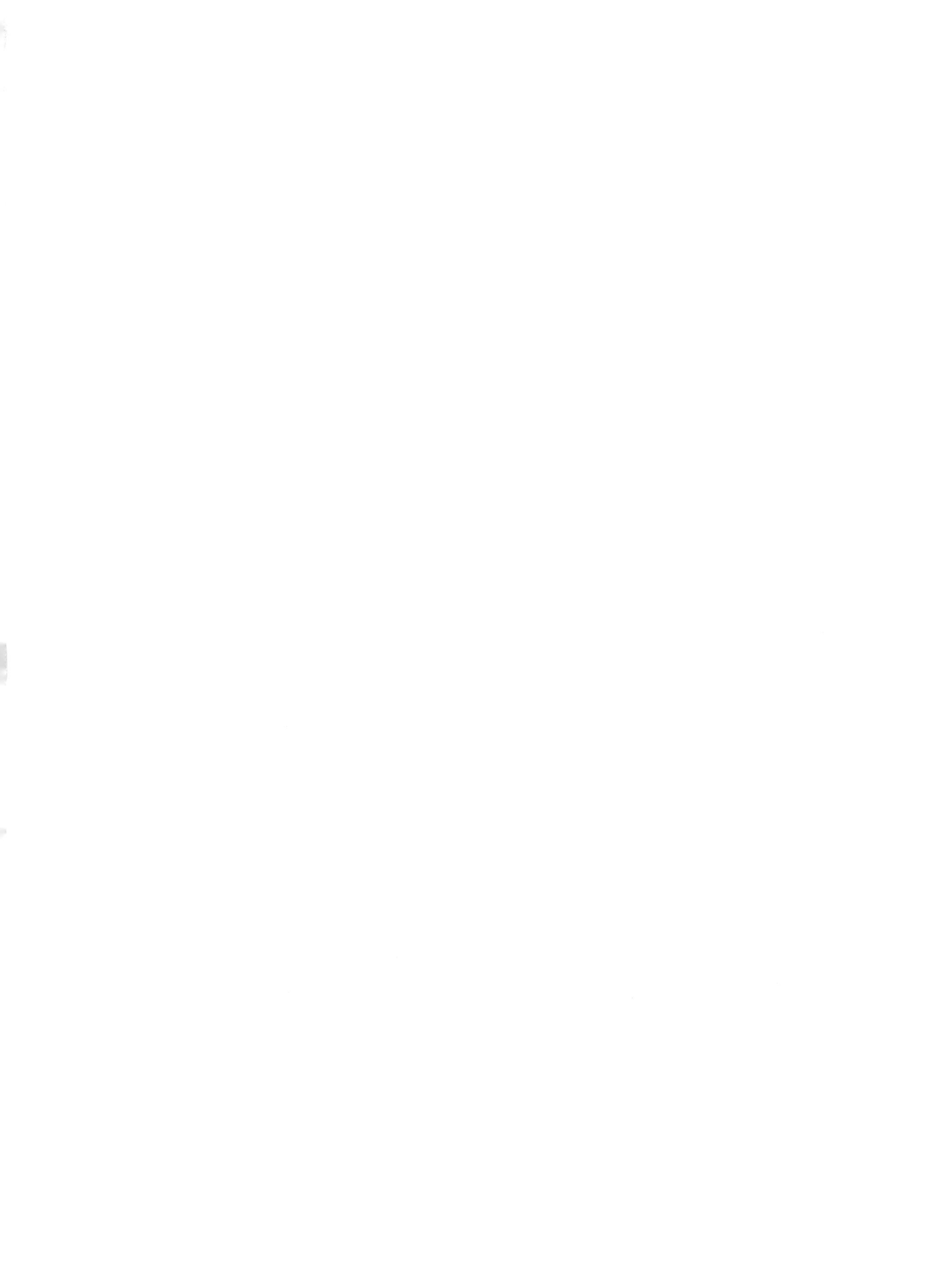

www.ingramcontent.com/pod-product-compliance
Lightning Source LLC
Chambersburg PA
CBHW050824180526
45159CB00004B/1785